START TO FINISH

DINGHY
SAILING

....

BARRY PICKTHALL

START TO FINISH

DINGHY
SAILING

....

BARRY PICKTHALL

WILEY ❖ NAUTICAL

Other Wiley Editorial Offices
John Wiley & Sons Inc., 111 River Street, Hoboken, NJ 07030, USA
Jossey-Bass, 989 Market Street, San Francisco
Wiley-VCH Verlag GmbH, Boschstr. 12, D-69
John Wiley & Sons Australia Ltd, 42 McDoug
John Wiley & Sons (Asia) Pte Ltd, 2 Clementi
John Wiley & Sons Canada Ltd, 6045 Freemo

Wiley also publishes its books in a variety of e
that appears in print may not be available in

Library of Congress Cataloging-in-Publication
Pickthall, Barry.
Dinghy sailing: start to finish / Barry Pickthall.
p. cm.
Includes index.
ISBN 978-0-470-69754-2 (pbk.: alk. paper)
1. Dinghies. 2. Sailing. I. Title.
GV811.6.P53 2009
797.124--dc22
2008047075
British Library Cataloguing in Publication Data
A catalogue record for this book is available from the British Library

ISBN: 978-0-470-69754-2

Design and typeset by PPL Ltd
Illustrations by Greg Filip/PPL
Printed and bound by SNP Leefung Printers Ltd, China

This book is printed on acid-free paper responsibly manufactured from sustainable forestry in which at least two trees are planted for each one used for paper production.

Contents

Getting started

I remember my introduction to sailing. My three young brothers and I and were on a family day out at Windsor, with a picnic by the river, watching people messing about in boats. Driving back home, we stopped at a garage to fill up, and my Dad, who was not normally prone to whims, spied this small sailing dinghy for sale on the forecourt – and bought it!

What we knew collectively about sailing could have been written on a postage stamp. The nearest Dad had come to getting afloat before had been when he had got his feet wet during the D-Day landings. None of us had even been on a car ferry, let alone a boat. Yet this insignificant little dinghy was to have a life-defining effect on us all. I went on to spend my whole career reporting on watersports; Russell, my youngest brother, went on to become a sailmaker and winning crewmember of a Whitbread Round-the-World Race yacht; another became a professional boatbuilder, and the fourth joined the Royal Navy.

Sailing is like that. You either love it or loathe it. There are no half measures, and once bitten, you will never want to be far from the water's edge again.

Buying a boat on a whim is not the best start. What little knowledge we culled from buying a magazine soon told us that we had bought a dud, but we had great fun with her that first season exploring rivers and creeks. We also learned from experience what effect the pull of a weir can have on a boat, and the need to keep wine corks ready for when the boat's bungs got left at home!

There are far better and more rational ways to start sailing. Enrol on an introductory dinghy course at the UKSA or similar sailing school.

If you are a junior, many sailing schools and clubs run fun introductory sailing courses during school holidays.

Visit local sailing clubs in your area, look at the various types of boat they sail and ask if anyone needs a crew – invariably, someone will be short-handed. Then make a judgement on which club best meets your needs, join and learn the ropes there. Then, you can get experience and buy a class of boat that is sailed at the club at a later stage.

Sailing is a sport that is accessible to everyone from 5 to 95 and older. Disability is no handicap either. With audible compasses to guide the blind, sliding seats for paraplegics and wheelchair access or hoists now available on some yachts, everyone has the opportunity to get afloat. Go on, get your feet wet and give it a try.

Barry Pickthall

Basic
principles

Parts of the boat

No need to get too bogged down with nautical terms at this stage, but it helps to know the various parts of a dinghy and what they do.

- **Mainsail**
Sail attached to mast and boom.

- **Jib fairlead**
Adjustable lead for rope that controls the jib or headsail.

- **Side benches/buoyancy tank**
Seats that double as side buoyancy.

- **Port side**
Left hand side of the boat.

- **Gunwale**
Top edge of the boat.

- **Cockpit**
Crew area within the boat.

- **Toe straps**
To hook your feet under when sitting on the side deck.

- **Stern/transom**
Back end of the dinghy.

- **Transom drains**
Holes in transom to allow water to escape the cockpit after a capsize or flooding.

- **Removable rudder**
Foil to steer the dinghy, which pivots up when boat is being launched or beached.

- **Centreboard**
Foil that pivots from centreboard case to counter sideways force from the sails.

- **Thwart**
Central seat across the boat for crew to sit on.

- **Starboard side**
Right hand side of the boat.

- **Tiller extension**
Attached to the tiller by a universal joint, this extends the reach of the tiller to allow the helmsman to sit out and control the rudder.

- **Hull**
Outer shell of the boat.

- **Tiller**
Used to steer the boat.

- **Mast**

- **Jib**
  Foresail.

- **Forestay**
  Forward wire holding up the mast.

- **Bow**
  The stem or front end of the boat.

- **Spinnaker chute**
  Launch and recovery tube for the spinnaker (used when sailing downwind).

- **Gooseneck**
  Hinged connection linking boom to mast.

- **Foredeck/bow buoyancy tank**
  Buoyancy to keep the bow afloat when boat is flooded.

- **Shrouds**
  Side wires holding up the mast.

- **Centreboard case**
  Casing that houses and supports the pivoting centreboard.

- **Mainsheet traveller**
  System to control mainsail angle.

- **Inspection hatch**
  Watertight hatch to check for water ingress in buoyancy tanks. (Keep shut when sailing.)

- **Side deck**
  Shaped to sit out and balance the boat against the heeling force of the wind.

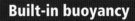

Built-in buoyancy

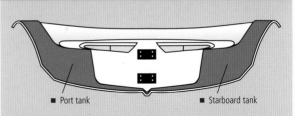

- Port tank   ■ Starboard tank

Buoyancy tanks (or inflatable bags) are designed to keep the dinghy afloat and on an even keel when capsized or flooded.

Parts of the boat

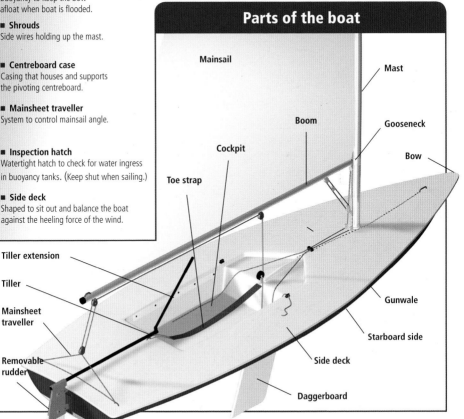

Mainsail

Mast

Boom

Gooseneck

Cockpit

Bow

Toe strap

Tiller extension

Tiller

Mainsheet traveller

Gunwale

Removable rudder

Starboard side

Side deck

Daggerboard

The rig

Modern dinghies are equipped either with a Bermuda rig, with jib and mainsail designed to interact like the slats of an aeroplane wing, or una rigged like the Laser single-hander.

■ Head
Top corner of sail.

■ Luff
Front edge of sail.

■ Roach
Curved edge to top third of sail supported by battens.

■ Head
Top corner of sail.

UKSA

■ Jib
Smaller foresail attached to a 'tack fitting' at the bow and hoisted at the front of the boat.

■ Forestay
Forward wire holding up the mast.

■ Luff
Front edge of sail.

■ Spreader
Lateral bar to provide lateral support and control curvature of mast bend.

■ Shroud
Wire side stay to support mast.

■ Gnav
Multi-purchase upward vang system to control downward tension on the boom.

■ Tack
Front corner of sail.

■ Main boom

■ Foot
Bottom edge of sail.

■ Cunningham
Provides micro adjustment to the luff of sail.

■ Gooseneck
Hinged connection linking mast and boom.

■ Mast step
Slot or socket to hold bottom of mast in place.

■ Jib sheets
Twin ropes attached to the clew to set jib to the correct angle to the wind.

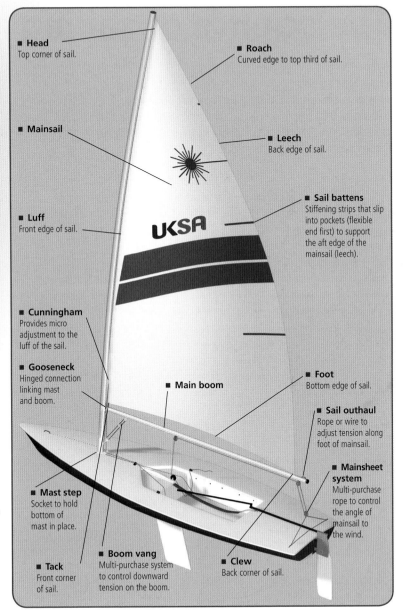

Mainsail
Larger sail set on the mast and boom.

Leech
Back edge of sail.

Sail battens
Stiffening strips that slip into pockets (flexible end first) to support the aft edge of the mainsail (leech). Full-length battens are often used to induce curvature into the top of the mainsail, with shorter battens supporting the lower part of the sail.

Halyards
Wire or rope lines to hoist the sails up the mast.

Foot
Bottom edge of sail.

Sail outhaul
Rope or wire to adjust tension along foot of mainsail.

Clew
Back corner of sail.

Mainsheet system
Multi-purchase rope to control the angle of mainsail to the wind.

Head
Top corner of sail.

Mainsail

Luff
Front edge of sail.

Cunningham
Provides micro adjustment to the luff of the sail.

Gooseneck
Hinged connection linking mast and boom.

Mast step
Socket to hold bottom of mast in place.

Tack
Front corner of sail.

Boom vang
Multi-purchase system to control downward tension on the boom.

Roach
Curved edge to top third of sail.

Leech
Back edge of sail.

Sail battens
Stiffening strips that slip into pockets (flexible end first) to support the aft edge of the mainsail (leech).

Main boom

Foot
Bottom edge of sail.

Sail outhaul
Rope or wire to adjust tension along foot of mainsail.

Mainsheet system
Multi-purchase rope to control the angle of mainsail to the wind.

Clew
Back corner of sail.

The science of sailing

The sight of a 747 jumbo jet coming slowly into land with wheels dangling and wings extended always leaves me in awe. How can something weighing as much as 380 tonnes fly so slowly – and not fall out of the sky? The answer is the same as that to the common question about sailing: How can a sailboat sail as close as 40° to the wind?

It is all about aerodynamics and the pressure differentials on one side of a wing, compared to the other. An aeroplane wing has more curvature on its upper surface. As it moves forward, the airflow streaming across has to travel faster over a longer distance to meet up with the air flowing along the flatter lower surface. This difference in speed leads to a drop in pressure on the upper surface, which results in lift. The faster the plane's speed the greater this becomes, to the point where the differential in pressure between the upper and lower sections of the wing is sufficient to raise the weight of the plane off the ground.

The same happens over the surface of a sail. The airflow across the back or leeward side, travels faster than the air flowing across the windward side. The resulting pressure differentials create the lift that drives the boat forward.

This force within the sail would drive the boat sideways were it not for the lateral resistance of the boat's daggerboard or centreboard. The best demonstration of this is to hold a knife blade in water and move it about, first up and down, and then sideways, when you will feel the lateral resistance. It is the balance in design between the sails and

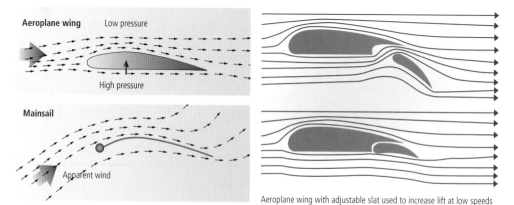

Aeroplane wing with adjustable slat used to increase lift at low speeds

shape of the hull that determines the efficiency with which a boat sails to windward.

A Thames barge and a Dutch botter are similar cargo carriers, shaped like bricks with inefficient leeboards that pivot down outside the side of the hull. As a result, sailors would rest up and wait for a fair wind rather than waste time attempting to buck into it.

By contrast, a modern dinghy like the Laser Bahia sails very efficiently to windward, providing the crew position their weight to balance out the heeling force of the wind. This efficiency is enhanced by the jib or forward sail, which induces a slot effect in the same way that extending slats on a plane wing improves lift coefficient at slow speeds when taking off and landing. Airflow narrows and accelerates through the 'slot' between jib and mainsail, improving the lift coefficient. The jib channels the air through the slot between the fore and aft sails, speeding the flow around the back of the mainsail to further improve the pressure differential between the windward and leeward sides.

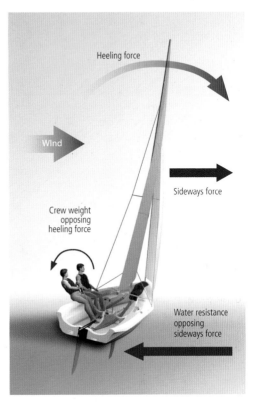

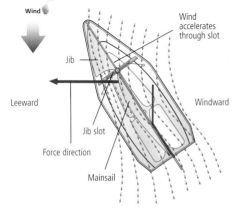

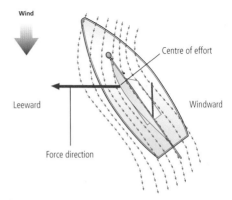

Centre of effort

Centre of lateral resistance

Centre of effort

A sailing dinghy is so well balanced that it is quite possible to alter course by adjusting the sails alone. Indeed, given the right conditions, instructors at the UKSA will often take students out in a dinghy without a rudder, to show them how they can vary the centre of effort within the sail plan. They learn that by letting the jib out (and moving the centre of effort aft) makes the boat point closer to the wind. Conversely, releasing the mainsail and sheeting in the jib moves the centre of effort forward and makes the boat bear away from the wind.

The centre of effort is a point within the sail plan where, if it was a card cut-out, could be balanced on the tip of a pin. This centre point within the rig must be in balance with the centre of resistance of the hull, a point on the centreboard. The closer these two points are on a vertical plane the better the balance will be.

Apparent wind

Apparent wind is the actual flow of air acting on the sail as the boat moves forward, and differs in speed and direction from the true or prevailing wind experienced by a stationary observer. The apparent wind is an important factor, when determining the angle that a dinghy will sail towards the wind. The faster the boat travels, the further the apparent wind angle moves forward and the greater its velocity. Wind indicators on the boat measure apparent wind. Stationary indicators such as flags show the true wind.

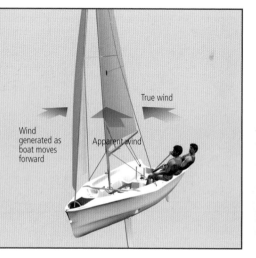

True wind

Wind generated as boat moves forward

Apparent wind

Driving force of the wind

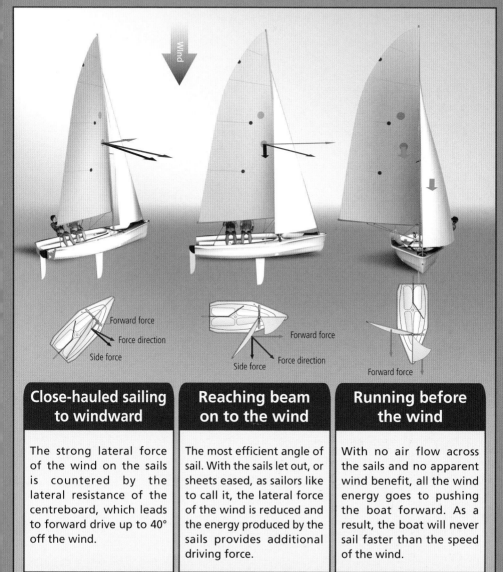

Wind

Forward force
Force direction
Side force

Forward force
Force direction
Side force

Forward force

Close-hauled sailing to windward

The strong lateral force of the wind on the sails is countered by the lateral resistance of the centreboard, which leads to forward drive up to 40° off the wind.

Reaching beam on to the wind

The most efficient angle of sail. With the sails let out, or sheets eased, as sailors like to call it, the lateral force of the wind is reduced and the energy produced by the sails provides additional driving force.

Running before the wind

With no air flow across the sails and no apparent wind benefit, all the wind energy goes to pushing the boat forward. As a result, the boat will never sail faster than the speed of the wind.

Points of sail

When sailing, the strength and direction of the wind are all-important. Look around you and see which way flags are flying. You can also feel the wind and sense its direction by turning your face. Your ears are highly tuned to sensing wind, as well as sound. When you change from one point of sail to another, the sails, centreboard and crew positions must also be adjusted to match the dinghy's balance and heading towards or away from the wind.

■ **Close-hauled: Sailing about 45° from the wind**
This is beating to windward with sails sheeted in hard, centreboard fully down to resist the sideways force of the wind on the sails, and crew weight out on the windward side to balance the boat.

Close -hauled

Close reach

Beam reach

Nc
zc

Wind

■ **Broad reach: 120–160° from the wind**

Broad reach

Training run

Run

■ **Run: 175–180° from the wind**
Sailing directly downwind either on port or starboard gybe. Sails are eased right out, the jib can be set on the opposite side to the mainsail (goose-winged) to project greater area to the wind, centreboard is fully raised and crew weight is spread across the boat.

■ Head to wind

This is the no-go zone and extends about 45° either side of the oncoming wind direction. Turn too high into the wind and the sails will start to flap, the boat will slow and eventually drift backwards. The only way to make progress is to sail at about 45° either side of the wind with sails sheeted in hard, and make a zigzag course. This is called beating to windward.

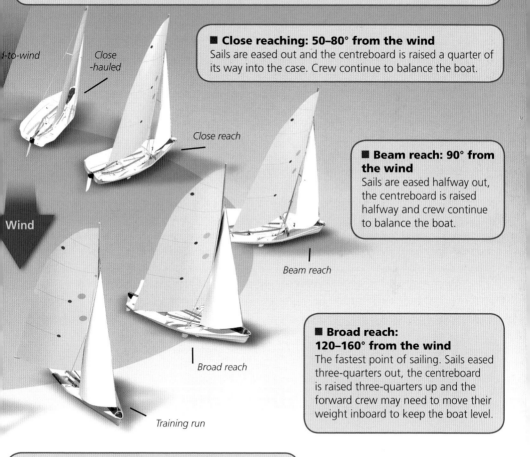

I-to-wind

Close-hauled

■ Close reaching: 50–80° from the wind

Sails are eased out and the centreboard is raised a quarter of its way into the case. Crew continue to balance the boat.

Close reach

■ Beam reach: 90° from the wind

Sails are eased halfway out, the centreboard is raised halfway and crew continue to balance the boat.

Wind

Beam reach

Broad reach

■ Broad reach: 120–160° from the wind

The fastest point of sailing. Sails eased three-quarters out, the centreboard is raised three-quarters up and the forward crew may need to move their weight inboard to keep the boat level.

Training run

■ Training run: 170° from the wind

The safest angle for novices to sail downwind. Sails are eased right out, centreboard is fully raised and crew weight is spread across the boat.

Choosing a dinghy

Resist the impulse to buy the first dinghy that takes your fancy, and get some experience either at a sailing school or a club before jumping in with both feet.

Our first family dinghy, bought on impulse from a garage forecourt, was our pride and joy for the first month. We soon learned how unsuitable it was!

Once you know the basics, you will have so much more idea of the type of boat best suited to your skill level and the area you want to sail. If you are joining a club, then selecting one of their classes will introduce you to a group of like-minded enthusiasts who will be only too pleased to offer help and advice – until you start beating them around the race course! If you prefer a boat to mess about in and tow to various venues behind the car, then you need one that is lighter than the towing vehicle, easy to launch and recover, and simple to rig.

Trapeze-rigged dinghies offer high performance, but only for those with the experience and agility to manage them.

Sailing a single-hander is the fastest way to learn, giving the steepest learning curve. The UKSA will usually put beginnrs in Picos or Laser Radial dinghies as a first option. The boats selected by the UKSA as sailing primers provide a good basis on which to categorize and judge other classes.

Laser Bahia

The Laser Bahia is a modern, stable, general-purpose family dinghy that can be sailed, rowed or motored. This low-maintenance, roto-moulded Jo Richards design even has a removable cool box for family outings. She is an ideal first boat to learn to sail in, having plenty of room for two crew and an instructor. Add a gennaker and trapeze, and it is easy to upgrade performance for racing.

Length:	15ft	4.6m
Beam:	6ft	1.8m
Mainsail:	113sq.ft	10.5sq.m
Jib:	40sq.ft	3.75sq.m
Gennaker:	150sq.ft	14sq.m
Mast:	20.5ft	6.29m
Weight:	386lb	175kg
Crew:		2-5

Laser 2000

The Laser 2000 is a popular two-person club racer with the ability to carry a third person when cruising. This Phil Morrison designed GRP-constructed dinghy is a strict one-design class and comes with hi-spec racing rig and gennaker.

Length:	14.4ft	4.44m
Beam:	6ft	1.85m
Mainsail:	93sq.ft	8.66sq.m
Jib:	35sq.ft	3.04sq.m
Gennaker:	109sq.ft	10.12sq.m
Mast:	20ft	6.1m
Weight:	362lb	164kg
Crew:		2-3

Vago

The Laser Vago is a high performance two-person racing dinghy designed by Jo Richards. The low-maintenance polyethylene tri-skin foam sandwich moulded hull has two rig options with a hi-spec racing rig* matched with a trapeze. The Vago can be sailed with one or two crew.

Length:	14ft	4.2m
Beam:	5ft	1.56m
Mainsail:	81sq.ft 100sq.ft*	7.56sq.m 9.31sq.m*
Jib:	29.9sq.ft	2.78sq.m
Gennaker:	130sq.ft 150sq.ft*	14sq.m 12.07 sq.m*
Mast:	20ft	6.19m
Weight:	275lb	125kg
Crew:		1-2

Bug

A junior trainer that doubles as a tender. The Bug, designed by Jo Richards, has the versatility to accommodate an adult or up to two youngsters in sailing trim – and a whole load more when under outboard power or rowed. Mass-produced in polyethylene, this dinghy weighs only 101lb (46kg) and is available with a standard or performance rig.

Length:		8.5ft	2.60m
Beam:		4.25ft	1.30m
Mainsail:			
	Standard	41sq.ft	3.8sq.m
	Performance	57sq.ft	5.3sq.m
Mast:			
	Standard	12.5ft	3.84m
	Performance	15ft	4.47m
Weight:		101lb	46kg
Crew:			1 adult or up to 2 juniors

Optimist

The Optimist dinghy has become the universal junior primer with large fleets spread across the world. Designed in 1947 by Clark Mills to be built from two sheets of plywood, the vast majority are now moulded. The boat has a simple gaff sail and is easily transported on a roof rack. This is the class that many Olympic medalists cut their racing teeth in, including 4-time British medalist Ben Ainslie.

Length:	7.75ft	2.36m
Beam:	3.75ft	1.12m
Mainsail:	35sq.ft	3.3sq.m
Mast:	7.5ft	2.26m
Weight:	275lb	125kg
Crew:		1

Pico

The Laser Pico is an entry-level beach dinghy available with a standard or sport rig and capable of being sailed single-handed or two up. Designed by Jo Richards with a self-draining cockpit, these mass-produced dinghies are roto-moulded in three-layer polyethylene.

Length:	11.5ft	3.5m
Beam:	4.75ft	1.43m
Mainsail: Standard Racing	55sq.ft 68sq.ft	5.14sq.m 6.33sq.m
Jib:	11.7sq.ft	1.09sq.m
Mast:	18ft	5.54m
Weight:	198lb	90kg
Crew:		1-2

Laser

The Laser is a strict one-design single-hander with three rig sizes that provide juniors with a step progression to racing right up to Olympic level. With close to 200,000 Lasers sailing worldwide, this popular GRP dinghy was designed by Bruce Kirby to provide close competition and focus on individual skills and fitness.

Length:	13.78ft	4.2m
Beam:	4.56ft	1.39m
Mainsail:		
Olympic	75.99sq.ft	7.06sq.m
Radial	62sq.ft	5.76sq.m
4.7	50.59sq.ft	4.7sq.m
Mast:	19.35ft	5.9m
Weight:	130lb	58.97kg
Crew:		1-2

Laser 4000

The Laser 4000 is a high performance two-person, one-design, trapeze racing dinghy with an adjustable hiking rack and corrector system designed to equalize the effect of crew weight and height. Slighter crews race with the racks fully extended and corrector weights added to equal the weight and leverage of bigger crews who sail with the racks set further inboard.

Length:	15ft	4.64m
Beam:	4.9ft - 7.5ft	1.5m - 2.3m
Mainsail:	116sq.ft	10.8sq.m
Jib:	42sq.ft	3.9sq. m
Gennaker:	184sq.ft	17.1sq.m
Mast:	23ft	7.1m
Weight:	328lb	149kg
Crew:		2

Dart 16

The Dart 16 catamaran was designed by Reg White and Yves Loday to be handled by an inexperienced crew. The hulls are mass-produced from three-layer polyethylene foam sandwich and have a skeg at the stern, which negates the need for daggerboards, allowing the boat to be sailed straight up the beach. The X racing version featured here has twin trapezes and a larger sail area.

Length:	15ft	4.64m
Beam:	7.5ft	2.3m
Mainsail:	112sq.ft	10.4sq.m
Jib:	29sq.ft	2.7sq.m
Gennaker:	124sq.ft	11.53sq.m
Mast:	24.5ft	7.5m
Weight:	313lb	142kg
Crew:		2

Transporting dinghies

Car roof or luggage rack

If the dinghy is light enough, like an Optimist, Pico or Laser, then the simplest mode of transport is to carry it on the car roof rack, and lash the mast, boom and launching trolley on top. The boat should be carried inverted so that the weight is spread across the deck or gunwales and the aerodynamics do not adversely affect the handling characteristics of the car.

❶ Invert the dinghy on its trolley and lift it upside down onto the car roof rack.

Tip

Lifting the boat up on your own is **not recommended**, especially if you want to put your back into sailing later in the day.

❹ ...then tie off the tails with a half-hitch to guard against the straps coming undone.

❷ Balance the hull on the roof rack with minimal overhang at the back of the car.

❸ Tie the boat down on the roof rack securely using adjustable straps...

❺ Tie the mast and boom sections to the inverted trolley, pad out the chocks and lift on top of the boat.

❻ Tie the trolley down. The bow rope, attached to the car tow hook, stops the boat moving from side to side.

Towing

The simplest way to tow, launch and recover a dinghy is on a combi trailer. This combines a simple road trailer with a launching trolley, and avoids the problem of corroded wheel bearings caused when the road trailer is immersed in water. These integral trailers are no more expensive than purchasing a trailer and launching trolley separately, and the supporting chocks can be purpose-made to fit the boat.

NEVER immerse the road trailer wheels in water – especially if the bearings are hot. Tie down or remove all loose items in the boat.

Towing tips

❶ Ensure the trailer is loaded slightly front heavy to avoid it 'snaking' out of control when braking or at speed.

❹ Tie the mast to the mast support at the front of the trailer and secure the foot to the transom bar or set inside a bucket against the transom to avoid damage to the boat.

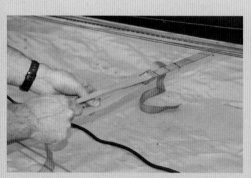

② Tie the boat and trolley down securely using adjustable straps or rope tensioned with a 'Lorry Driver's' hitch.

③ Tie down to strong points on the trailer.

⑥ Lock the jockey wheel in place.

⑤ Secure the front of the boat to both the trolley and trailer.

⑦ The lighting bar should extend the full width of the boat.

Packing away

After sailing there are a few essential chores to keep the boat in tip-top condition – and ready to sail again.

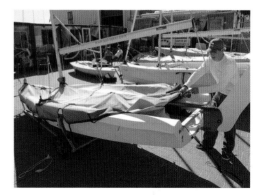

- Remove the bungs and wash the boat down with fresh water, paying particular attention to all moving parts, washing out any dirt and salt.
- De-rig the boat, and reattach shackles so that they don't get lost.
- Tension and tie off the halyards so that they don't rattle against the mast.

A cover protects the dinghy from the elements and hinders pilfering. Always tie the boat down to a secure point in the ground to stop it from being blown over in a gale.

- Allow sails to dry before rolling them up carpet-like along their luff, pulling out any creases as they form, before stowing in their bags.
- Open hatches to allow air to circulate, and drain any water from the buoyancy tanks.
- Disassemble the rudder and place the foil in its protective bag.
- If you have a removable daggerboard, this needs to be put away in its protective bag.
- Check for breakages or wear and make notes to repair or replace before your next sail.
- Tie the bow to the trolley and put the cover on, making sure it is well tied. A boat cover protects the dinghy from the elements and hinders 'borrowing' and pilfering.
- Tie the boat down to secure points in the ground to prevent it from being blown over.

Knots, ropes and running rigging

The best way to learn knots is to carry a piece of thin cord in your pocket and practise during quiet moments until you can do them with your eyes shut.

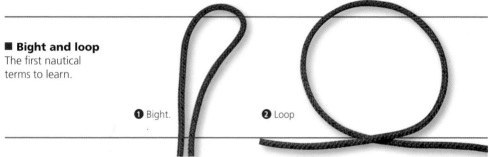

■ Bight and loop
The first nautical
terms to learn.

❶ Bight.

❷ Loop

Standing part

Working end

■ Reef knot
Used to tie two
lines of equal
thickness
together such
as reefing lines
and sail ties.
Remember the
rule: Left over
right. Right
over left.

❶ Bring the two ends
of the rope together,
cross left over right
and tuck under.

❷ Continuing with the
same end, cross right
over left and tuck under.

❸ Pull tight and check.

For an interactive
lesson, go to
**www.uksa.org/
knotmaster**
and master
5 knots
in 5 days.

**■ Figure-of
eight-knot**
Stopper knot tied into
the ends of sheets
and halyards to stop
them from running
out through a block
or sheet fairlead.

❶ Form a loop.

❶ Form a loop in the end of the rope.

❷ Form the loop (rabbit hole) to the size required, with the outer end upward and pass the working end up through the loop

■ Bowline

Ties a non-slip knot in the end of a rope. Used to form a secure loop in the end of a mooring line or to tie a sheet to the clew of a sail. Remember the adage: *The rabbit comes out of its hole, runs round the tree then goes back down the hole again.*

❸ Then round the back of the standing part...

❹ ...and back down through the small loop (rabbit hole).

❺ Pull the the working end through the small loop.

❻ Pull tight and check the tail is long enough not to pull out.

❷ Pass the end round the back of the standing part.

❸ Return the end through the loop.

❹ Pull tight.

■ Single sheet bend
Used to tie two lines
of unequal thickness
together such as sail ties.

① Form a bight in the thicker rope.

② Pass the end of the thinner rope
up through the bight and under.

③ Pass the end of the thinner rope
under its own standing part.

④ Pull tight.

■ Double sheet bend
A more secure
version of the single
sheet bend, and the
preferred method for
tying two disparate
sized mooring lines
together. A good
knot to tie a rope
of any thickness
to a rope loop.

① Form a bight in the thicker rope.

② Pass the end of the thinner rope
up through the bight and under.

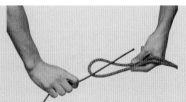

③ Pass the end of the thinner rope
under its own standing part and repeat.

④ Pull tight and check that the ends
exit on the same side of the knot.

■ Clove hitch
Used to attach a temporary line to a rail or ring.

❶ Easy to undo, so make sure you leave a long working end.

❷ Pass the working end around the object and back across itself.

❸ Form another half hitch.

❹ Pull tight.

■ Round turn and two half hitches
Used to attach a line to a post or ring. Easy to untie, even under load, so ideal for securing a mooring line or fenders.

❶ Pass the end round the back and form a half hitch.

❷ Repeat to form a second half hitch.

❸ Pull tight.

■ Coiling rope

Loose rope ends like halyard tails and mooring lines should be coiled and secured with the tail so that they are ready to be shaken out at a moment's notice.

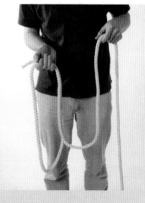

❶ Take the end of the rope in one hand, stretch it out with the other, twist it clockwise...

■ Cleating a rope

The OXO method of tying off a mooring line or halyard on a horn cleat.

❶ Take a full turn around the cleat.

❷ cross over in a figure-of-eight....

❸ ...and finish with a final turn around the cleat.

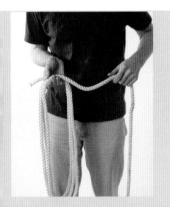

2 ...and transfer each loop to the first hand.

3 Once coiled, make several turns with the working end around the coils and feed through the top loop...

4 ...and pull tight.

■ Cam cleat

Pull the rope down through the twin spring-loaded cams and allow the load on the rope to hold it tight. To clear, simply pull the rope tail upwards.

■ Clam cleat

This simple cleat has no moving parts. Steer the rope into the jaws and allow the load on the rope to draw it down into the grooves and lock it. Works best with three-stranded ropes. To clear, simply pull the rope tail upwards.

Essential gear

After checking over your own protective clothing and buoyancy aid, the dinghy should have a safety check before going afloat.

Paddle: Stowed securely and within easy reach.

Safety equipment

Anchor and line. A small folding grapnel anchor takes up least space. Together with the line, which doubles as a towing warp, pack 4ft (1.2m) of chain to act as ground tackle and hold the anchor down. These must be stowed securely to prevent it falling out in the event of a capsize.

Towing rope: At least twice the length of the dinghy, and with a minimum breaking strain of twice the weight of boat and crew. Usually, 10mm thickness will suffice.

Bailer, sponge, waterproof charts, knife, spare rope and tape.

Waterproof bag
To carry mobile phone, water, energy drinks and bars. If you are cruising around, consider carrying spare clothing and personal items.

Buoyancy
Your dinghy may have built-in buoyancy tanks like the Laser Bahia.
Check inside the inspection hatches for any water, and sponge out.
Check that the hatches are watertight. A little Vaseline applied around the opening will stop ingress.
Buoyancy bags: If your boat has air bags, check that they are fully inflated.

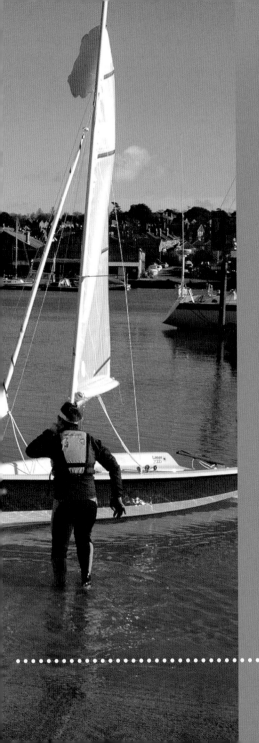

Preparing
to sail

What to wear

You are going to get wet, so be prepared...to enjoy it!

Unless you are sailing in the tropics, wearing the right clothing to keep you warm and dry is the first requisite to maximizing that enjoyment.

There is a wide variety of specialist clothing available, but for dinghy sailors the two best options are a neoprene wetsuit, or warm underclothes overcoated with a drysuit or drytop with rubber sealed collar and cuffs.

The other priority is a buoyancy aid or, for non-swimmers, a fully inflated lifejacket that will keep you afloat with your head above water in the event of a dunking. Self inflating lifejackets are not suitable for dinghy sailing because they inflate whenever they get wet, and not just when you fall overboard

Drysuit/Drytop

Unlike a wetsuit, the drysuit and drytop are designed to keep the body dry. They are particularly suited for use in cold waters and can be uncomfortable to wear in hot climates unless the membrane material has breathable properties like Goretex. Buy ones that are oversize to allow for warm polyester underclothes and ease of movement. Then they are also easy to get on and off.

The drysuit is a one-piece. The drytop is designed to be worn with hi-fit trousers which I find preferable, because you can take the top off when the weather is hot and sultry.

Wetsuit

The neoprene wetsuit helps to preserve body heat by trapping a layer of water against the skin, which is consequently warmed by body heat and acts as an insulator. To be efficient, the suit must be a snug fit otherwise the warm water will escape, taking the body heat with it. The latest rubber materials now incorporate merino wool and titanium fibres and other insulants, adding to warmth and minimizing thickness to allow for easier movement. These buoyant suits are available in full length, shortie and long-john styles.

This one-piece drysuit has a rubber seal around the neck.

Waterproof zip across the torso.

Rubber seals around the cuffs.

The drytop relies on a velcroed rubber seal around the neck...

Two types of dinghy dry wear. Left is a one-piece suit with rubber seals. Right is a drytop jacket worn in conjunction with hi-fit waterproof trousers.

...and a similar arrangement on the cuffs to stop water ingress.

Dinghy boots

There is the choice of neoprene rubber boots with moulded non-slip soles to keep the feet warm and provide good grip, or more hard-wearing boots worn over the latex rubber socks of a drysuit. Buy these oversize to allow for the thickness of the socks.

Hats

Since more than 30% of body heat is lost through the head, a hat is important. Beanies or balaclavas are good in cold weather and a baseball cap will keep the sun out of your eyes in the summer, but fit a restraining strap – they have a habit of flying away in the wind.

Gloves

Extended exposure to water softens the skin, so a good pair of fingerless sailing gloves not only gives you good grip, but still allows you to tackle fiddly tasks like undoing knots and shackles.

Buoyancy aids/lifejackets

These are available to match all shapes and sizes. They are even available for pets. The buoyancy aid or personal flotation device (PFD) is a buoyancy aid and not a life-saving device. They are popular with dinghy sailors because they are less restrictive, but non-swimmers should always wear a lifejacket, which is designed to keep your head above water.

Make sure that your choice is type-approved by your national standards authority, sized to match your body weight and fits comfortably over your sailing suit.

A buoyancy aid will typically have front and back closed-cell foam buoyancy to provide complete freedom of arm movement. These are available as a one-piece vest pulled on over the head or as a front zip jacket and will include a waist strap to prevent it from coming off in the water.

Buoyancy aids sold in the European Union are CE tested and approved. Sailing buoyancy aids are usually '50 newton class' flotation aids (CE code 393), providing a minimum of 50 N (11lb/15.5kg) of buoyant force. Some buoyancy aids classed as '100 N' have the force to flip a swimmer over onto their back, include a neck support and are usually worn by children or inexperienced swimmers.

In the USA, choose a buoyancy aid that is type-approved by the United States Coast Guard. Type II buoyancy aids are recommended for confident swimmers. 'Type III' Flotation Aids have 69N (15.5lb/17kg) of buoyant force and include a collar to keep the face of an unconscious person out of the water.

Left: Front-zip buoyancy aid. Right: One-piece buoyancy vest.

Rigging the boat

❶ Stepping the mast. This is a two-person task. Check that there are no electric cables overhead. Fit pennant to top of mast.

❷ Lift the mast up into wind. Having attached the shrouds to the chain plates, one person takes the weight of the mast on their shoulders and continues to steady the spar while the second crew hauls it upright by the forestay.

❸ Once upright attach forestay to bow, ensure mast is vertical in boat and check mast rake. Adjust shrouds to suit.

Setting up the rig

❶ Turn boat into wind.

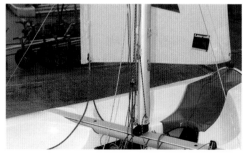

❷ Attach jib and hoist halyard, with second crew pulling on forestay to help tension halyard.

❸ Attach the jib sheets, lead through jib fairleads and back to the jib clew.

❹ Furl the jib by keeping tension on the sheet with one hand...

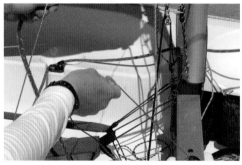

❺ ...haul in on the furling line.

❻ Jib fully furled.

❽ Connect boom to gooseneck.

❼ Insert the battens, thin end first into the batten pockets within the leech of the sail, making sure that they locate properly into their elasticated end stops within the pockets.

❾ Attach main halyard to top of mainsail

❿ with the self-locking knot

⓫ Feed mainsail luff into mast track while second person hauls on halyard.

⓬ Pull mainsail to top of mast (stop at black band), and tie off halyard.

⑬ Attach tack of mainsail (the tack strip is attached last.

⑭ Slide foot of mainsail into slot on boom.

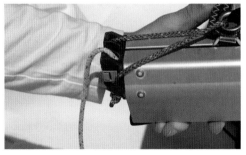

⑮ Attach clew outhaul.

⑯ Connect the boom gnav. Attach cunningham system to the luff of sail.

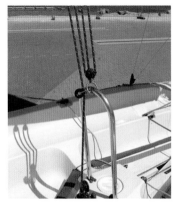

⑰ Attach mainsheet system and tie figure-of-eight stopper knot in end of sheet.

⑱ Fit rudder and tiller.

CHECK THE BUNGS!
You are now ready to sail.

The Laser, like many modern single-handed dinghies, is a supremely simple boat to set up.

1 Slot the two mast tubes together so that the arrows line up.

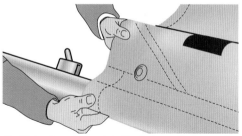

2 Slide the sleeved luff of the sail down the mast tube and check that the foot is in line with the gooseneck.

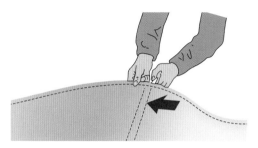

3 Insert the sail battens, thin end first, into the batten pockets, making sure that they locate properly into their elasticated end stops within the pockets.

4 Check that there are no electric cables overhead. Lift the mast up into the wind. When the mast is balanced, slot the foot into its hole in the foredeck.

5 Wheel the boat to the water's edge and turn the bows head to wind. Attach the gooseneck and the clew to the boom outhaul.

6 Tie a separate line through the clew tightly around the boom.

❼ Attach the vang assembly to the mast.

❽ Rig the outhaul through and cunningham adjustor through the blocks and down to their cleats on the deck.

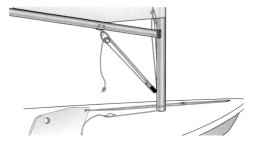

❾ Attach the daggerboard elastic retainer to the bow and lay board inside boat until after launching, so that it does not foul the vang.

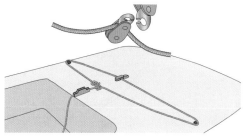

❿ Connect the boom and mainsheet traveller.

⓫ Rig the mainsheet. Fit the rudder, with the tiller under the rope traveller.

You are now ready to sail.

Launching

Beach or slipway launch

Tie a rope (termed a painter), of approximately the same length as the boat, to the bow.

■ **CHECK BUNGS ARE IN AND TRANSOM FLAPS ARE SHUT.**

Keeping the boat head to wind, either push or pull the trolley into the water (depending on the wind direction) until the dinghy floats clear. Keep hold of the painter.

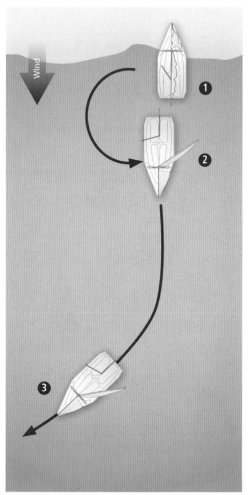

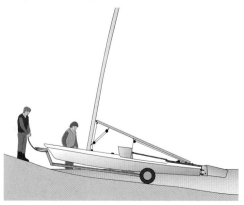

Second person holds bows into wind, clear of other users (or boat is tied up), and first person pulls the trolley out and leaves it above the high-water mark.

Launching from a beach with an offshore wind

❶ Check wind direction, turn the boat head to wind, hoist sails on land and launch the boat, ensuring that the the vang (GNAV) is slack and sheets are loose. Helm then holds boat while crew climbs in to balance the boat.

❷ Helm turns bows away from the wind, pushes off and climbs in, then pulls rudder downhaul to lock blade down. Crew pulls the centreboard down part way.

❸ Helm and crew set sails to suit course. YOU ARE SAILING.

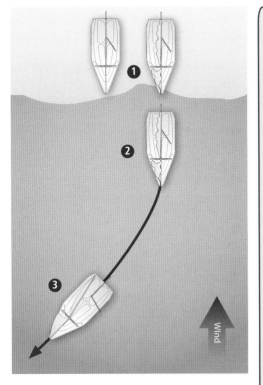

Launching from a beach with an onshore wind

❶ Check wind direction, turn the boat head to wind and rig the sails on land.

Launch the boat bow first, by leading the trolley into the water and removing it once the dinghy is afloat.

❷ Helm climbs in and pulls the centreboard part way down and pulls the rudder downhaul to lock blade down. Crew then pushes the boat off and climbs in.

❸ Helm and crew pull in the sails and crew adjusts centreboard to stop sideways drift (leeway).

YOU ARE SAILING.

❶ A combination road/launching trailer allows you to launch the boat straight from the road trailer.

❷ NEVER allow the trailer bearings to get wet. This leads to internal corrosion and early failure of the bearings. Stop the trailer at the water's edge and use the trolley to launch the boat.

❸ Release the trolley lock and lift the bow handles so that the trolley slides easily over the stern rollers on the trailer. Reverse the operation when recovering the boat after sailing.

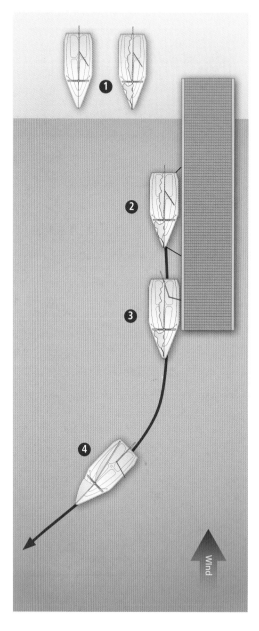

Pontoon launch with an onshore wind

1 Check wind direction, turn the boat head to wind and rig the sails on land.

- Check bungs are in and transom flaps are shut.

- Hold onto the painter and launch the boat into the water bow first,

2 Tie the boat to the pontoon. Helm climbs aboard, fits the rudder and pulls the centreboard down part way.

3 Crew unties the lines and pulls boat forward to the end of the pontoon, then steps aboard and pushes off.

4 Helm pulls in mainsail, crew sheets in jib and pulls down centreboard to stop sideways drift (leeway).

YOU ARE SAILING.

Tidal effect

- If you are leaving a deep-water pontoon, the tidal stream may have a significant effect if sailing at sea.

- Be careful that the tide does not carry you into another obstruction before you have gained steerage way.

- The same applies when sailing back onto the pontoon.

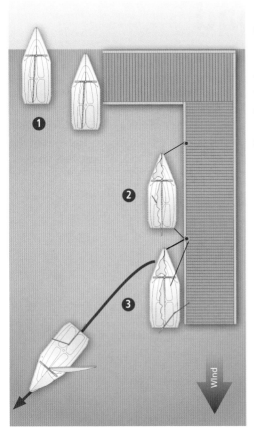

Pontoon launch with an offshore wind

❶ With the wind blowing in this direction, it is possible to hoist sails before launching the boat, but beginners might find it easier to do this later, once the boat is tied up alongside the pontoon.

- Check bungs are in and transom flaps are shut.
- Hold onto the painter and launch the boat into the water stern first, avoiding causing damage to the hull or flooding over the transom.

❷ Tie the boat to the pontoon so that it lies head to wind. Helm climbs aboard to hoist sails, fit the rudder and pull the centreboard down part way.

❸ Crew then releases the stern line and unties the painter, keeping one turn round the bollard. Maintaining tension on the tail to keep the bow close to the pontoon, crew then steps onboard.

❹ Check wind direction. Crew sets the jib on the starboard side to blow the bow round away from the pontoon, and releases the painter. Helmsman steers the boat round and ensures that the mainsail is free. Once the bow has swung through 45°, crew releases jib, sheets in on opposite side and adjusts centreboard to suit course. Helm trims mainsail.

YOU ARE SAILING.

Rules of the road

All vessels, from the smallest rowing tender to the largest supertanker, are governed by the same rules known as the International Regulations for The Prevention of Collisions at Sea or IRPCS. These 'rules of the road' take precedence over the International Yacht Racing Rules set by the International Sailing Federation (ISAF). Under the racing rules, vessels not racing are considered obstructions to be avoided using the IRPCS. So if you don't obey the rules, your competitors can protest you out of the race for offences against an innocent bystander!

Sailing with other dinghies

If you are sailing with other dinghies there are three rules that cover most eventualities.

▪ **Vessels on port tack give way to vessels on starboard tack.**

The rules define the tack you are on as the opposite side to the one on which you are carrying your boom, so if the boom is on the port side you are on starboard tack. If you are not sure if the other boat is on starboard (perhaps their spinnaker is in the way) then keep clear anyway.

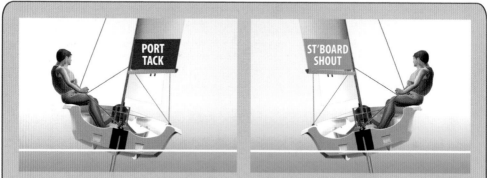

Mark the boom

One easy reminder as to which tack you are on is to mark the boom where the helm can see it clearly from their normal steering position on the opposite side of the boat. Inscribe with an indelible pen on the left hand side of the boom PORT and on the right hand side ST'BOARD. Alternatively, place a red sticker on the port side, and green one on the starboard side.

■ **An overtaking vessel gives way to the vessel being overtaken.**

This means if you are overtaking a power boat in your dinghy you must keep clear.

■ **If two sailing boats are on the same tack then the windward boat keeps clear.**

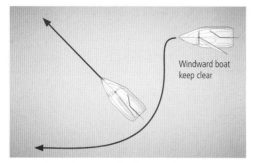

Windward boat keep clear

This is because the leeward boat is closer to that dangerous lee shore. Again, if you are unsure which tack the other boat is on, then keep clear.

An easy way to remember this is a POW (Prisoner of War) has no rights – so if you are a P, O or W (Port, Overtaking, or Windward boat) you have no rights and must keep clear.

Sailing in a harbour

Most vessels in harbour will drive on the right (as the rules tell them to) and if the prevailing conditions allow, so should the sailing dinghy. However, when sailing upwind in a river or harbour entrance, you must be aware of vessels coming in the opposite direction, as well as from behind. Keep a careful watch all around, and give plenty of warning to both your crew and other boats around whenever you plan to tack. If a potential collision develops, make your intention obvious by making a large alteration in course. If you meet a large vessel in a narrow channel or harbour think about your actions early in relation to the wind direction, tide or current flow and other vessels in your area. Options may include timing your entrance to the harbour so as to miss the shipping, sailing alongside or picking up a mooring till the traffic has passed, sailing into shallow water or out of the main channel, or even just turning around and sailing away from the danger.

One classic mistake is to get too close to the bow of an oncoming vessel, forcing them out into the channel and trapping you between them and the side of the harbour. Remember that not all power boaters are aware of the mechanics of tacking upwind and don't understand why you are zigzagging in front of them.

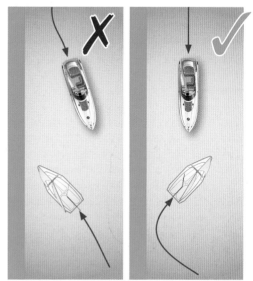

Dinghy trapped between powerboat and wall. *Time your tack to let the powerboat through.*

Harbour authorities may have local bylaws which supersede the IRPCS inside their jurisdiction, such as allowing fishing boats to trawl in the harbour, banning the use of spinnakers, or giving commercial shipping absolute rights over all types of pleasure craft. It is important to get the relevant information from the harbour office or Harbour Master's staff before setting out.

Sailing in Open Water

The rule book defines many different kinds of vessels and the actions they should take in relation to each other. Dinghies are defined as sailing vessels and come quite a long way down the pecking order of who should give way to whom. Indeed, the only other water users that give way to sailing dinghies are seaplanes, hovercraft and power-driven vessels that have nothing influencing where they can go. See the list of vessels that dinghies must give way to and the shapes or flags that tell us why.

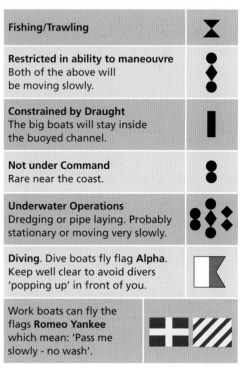

Fishing/Trawling	
Restricted in ability to maneouvre Both of the above will be moving slowly.	
Constrained by Draught The big boats will stay inside the buoyed channel.	
Not under Command Rare near the coast.	
Underwater Operations Dredging or pipe laying. Probably stationary or moving very slowly.	
Diving. Dive boats fly flag **Alpha**. Keep well clear to avoid divers 'popping up' in front of you.	
Work boats can fly the flags **Romeo Yankee** which mean: 'Pass me slowly - no wash'.	

Shipping

Keep a watchful eye open for ships. Their speed can be very deceptive. Even in restricted waters, these vessels can be making as much as 15 knots in order to keep steerageway during turns. That means they will be bearing down on you at the rate of 1 mile every 4 minutes, so a ship that was on the horizon one minute can be a real hazard within 10–15 minutes. Ships may also be constrained to the deep-water channel and unable to alter course to avoid you. Remember that visibility from the ship's bridge is very restricted. A dinghy will often 'disappear' from the view of the pilot and helm when more then half a mile ahead, so don't even consider crossing ahead unless you are absolutely sure you can get across in time. When crossing a channel, sail well within your personal limits – do not put yourself in a position of capsizing in front of an approaching ship. Large vessels will generate a temporary wind shadow so be aware of what the tide will do to you if you lose sail power when they pass you. Commercial ships are busy earning a living. Dinghy sailors on the other hand, are out there for enjoyment, so be considerate and keep well out of the way if you can.

Sound signals

Power boats are fond of making sound signals as it is easy for them - they just press a button. Dinghy sailors normally don't have the signaling equipment necessary to draw attention to themselves, and can only communicate their intentions by using bold manoeuvres in good time.

The sound signals you are most likely to hear will be short (•) or long (-) blasts. Long tends to be more than 4 seconds

•	I am turning to starboard.
••	I am turning to port.
•••	I am slowing down or going backwards.
•••••	I am unclear of your intentions (and getting worried).
-	I am coming (possibly round a corner or under a bridge).

✓	Make your alteration in course early and obvious.
✓	Pass at a safe distance.
✓	If the ship gives five short blasts they are already worried about what you are doing.
✓	Avoid collisions at all costs.
✓	Use common sense.
✓	Port gives way to starboard.
✓	Windward boat keeps clear.
✓	Overtaking boat keeps clear.
✓	Treat shipping with respect.

Wind and tides

To start with, the outside elements of wind and tides can seem complex, but the telltale signs are all easy to read – once you know what to look for.

As UKSA senior instructor Richard Baggett likes to tell his students, "God gave you ears… to feel which way the wind is coming from. They are the best wind antennae you have, so use them!"

The first rule before going sailing is to check the local weather forecast and tides, which are readily available from the web, weather channels, harbour offices, and even SMS text to your mobile phone.

The second rule is to keep a weather eye out, looking for changes in wind strength or direction by monitoring flags, smoke stacks and other boats around you. The Mark 1 eyeball is an excellent forecasting tool if used regularly.

When the winds are offshore, the seas can be deceptively calm close inshore and require forethought when you return because they will involve beating into wind when heading back. Onshore winds can make it difficult to launch the boat and leave the shore through breaking waves and facing winds, but once out beyond the shelving beach, the waves will invariably lessen, and the wind direction will also make it much easier to return to shore later. Launching through breaking waves is not for the beginner however. If you must get afloat, head for calmer waters.

Tidal Height and Flow

Over approximately six and a half hours the height of tide rises to high water, and then over approximately the next six and a half hours falls to low water. This happens with monotonous regularity and is predicted to the minute by tide tables which can be obtained from nautical almanacs, sailing clubs, harbourmasters, and in many cases directly from the internet. Tides are caused by the interaction between the Sun, the Moon and the Earth. When the three bodies line up (with the new moon – Fig 1 – or the full moon – Fig 2) the Sun's and the Moon's gravity directly add to each other, and this causes spring tides, where the high water levels are relatively

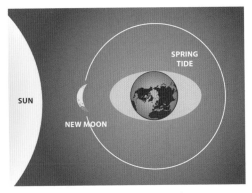

Fig 1: Gravity of moon and sun act together

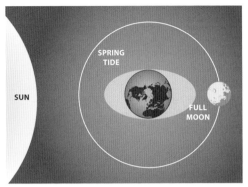

Fig 2: Gravity of moon and sun act together

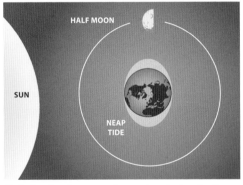

Fig 3: Gravity of moon and sun act against each other

high, and the low water levels are relatively low. Where the Sun and the Moon are at right angles relative to the Earth (half moon – Fig 3) their respective gravitational pulls are at right angles and therefore not directly adding to each other. This causes neap tides (Fig 5), where the high waters are not as high as at springs, and the low waters are not as low as at springs.

Apart from the obvious point that the height of tide decides which rocks are dangerous or not to the fragile bottom of a dinghy, the range of tide (the difference in height between high water and low water on a particular day) has a direct bearing on the rate of tidal flow. The time period of the tide is constant, so spring tides have faster rates than neap tides, because they have the same six and a half hours to move a greater volume of water along the coast. Logically, tide would flood in to high water, and then immediately turn and ebb towards low water – in practice, however, the turn of tidal flow can occur up to two hours before the relevant high or low water. This information can be obtained from tidal stream atlases, local sailors, sailing clubs and harbourmasters.

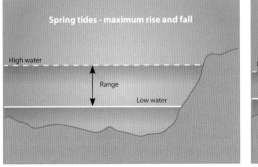

Fig 4

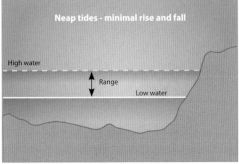

Fig 5

Inland Waterways

Inland, the flow or water on rivers will vary depending on recent rainfall levels. The flow is also much greater on the outside turns of the river and close to weirs, which should always be given a wide berth.

The Combination of Wind and Tide

Tidal rates can vary greatly – 2 knots is fairly average in some locations, and in narrow harbour entrances or gaps between islands it can reach 5 or 6 knots on a regular basis. This has a direct effect on where the journey goes and the sea state during it.

The sea state is generated mostly by the effect of the surface wind on the water. If there is wind with tide (Fig 6), then the sea state will be relatively smooth, and not so choppy. In wind over tide (Fig 7) scenarios this

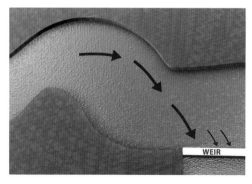

Water flow is greater on the outer curve. Beware of weirs.

can be quite different, with the waves much shorter and steeper, with a greater risk of capsizing, flooding and swamping.

If strong winds are forecast, it is important to know when the tide is flooding and ebbing, as that directly affects when the sea state goes from "Wheeee!"to "Heeelp!".

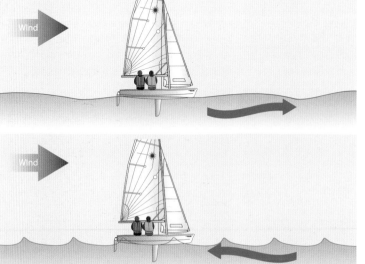

Fig 6. Wind with tide..

Fig 7. Wind against tide.

Perfect sailing conditions

Sailors competing in the 18ft Skiff World championship in Sydney Harbour, Australia, were treated to perfect sailing conditions. Here, the lack of cloud, hot sun and the onshore component of the prevailing winds helps to deliver a healthy sea breeze.

Telltale signs of the weather

Clouds – what are they and what do they mean?

As air passes over water moisture will be picked up by the air and carried in suspension. The amount of water carried and picked up depends to a large extent on the temperature of the air and the temperature of the water over which it flows. For many reasons this air may then rise or be cooled (or both) and moisture will come out of suspension in the form of water vapour, which is seen as clouds. The type of cloud formed depends on what is happening to the air from which it comes, so the clouds are a good indicator of what the weather is, or is about to be, doing.

There are four main categories of clouds:
Cirrus – a tuft or filament
Cumulus – the classic fluffy "Mr Men" Cloud
Stratus – layered cloud
Nimbus – rain bearing cloud (usually a darker more ominous grey)
There are many individual cloud types, the most common are as follows.

High clouds
Base heights of clouds between 18,000 and 45,000 feet (5,500 and 14,000 metres)

Cirrus
- Cirrocumulus
- Cirrostratus

Medium clouds
Base heights of clouds between 6,500 and 18,000 feet (2,000 and 5,500 metres)

Alto
- Altocumulus
- Altostratus
- Nimbostratus

Low clouds
Base heights of clouds surface to 6,500 feet (2,000 metres)

- Cumulonimbus   Cumulus   Stratus
  - Stratocumulus

Cirrus: long feathery filaments of ice crystals often associated with tufts known as "mares' tails". These are typically associated with the approach of a frontal system, meaning that changeable weather is on the way in the next 24 hours.

Cirrocumulus: known as a "mackerel sky" they are composed of collections of high altitude ice crystals and look like rippled sand on a beach. These are typically associated with the approach of a frontal system.

Cirrostratus: a more continuous high level layer of ice crystals, again associated with an approaching frontal system. This cloud may give rise to a halo around the sun and the moon.

Altocumulus: thin, broken up fluffy clouds, they are the next indicator after the cirrus clouds that a frontal system, and therefore rain, is on the way in the next 12 hours or so.

Altostratus: a thin, reasonably consistent layer of cloud through which the sun will shine weakly. There will be patches of darker grey in it, and this is an imminent precursor to rain and the arrival of a front.

Nimbostratus: a darker, heavier version of stratus clouds, with identifiable features that can hang off the base of the main formation almost like large sacks of rain waiting to fall. Any precipitation is likely to be heavy, with some unpredictable wind shifts and gusts on the edges of these showers.

Stratus: a most depressing low, uniform grey layer of cloud with few identifiable features. There will be scattered drizzle and light rain under these, and they generally occur at the end of fronts or in the warm sector of a frontal system.

Cumulus: individual white or light grey fluffy clouds, often seen along coastlines in the afternoon as a result of warm air rising as the day heats up or in the relatively dry air following the passing of a frontal system. They are a good indicator of fair weather.

Stratocumulus: layered cumulus clouds, generally white or light grey in patches. These are not threatening, and generally the worst that will happen is the occasional shower.

Cumulonimbus: these clouds are typically associated with cold fronts, often forming line squalls just in front of them. They are typically low based but can reach up as high as 40,000 feet, and are very energetic, dark and forbidding formations, generating rain, hail, thunder and lightning, as well as unpredictable strong squalls around their edges and underneath them. They can be embedded in layers of stratocumulus and can be spotted by their extremely dark bases and characteristic anvil top.

Red sky at night, sailor's delight: this saying is often true – if a frontal system has passed over from west to east, as is generally the case, then the setting sun in the west will light up the clouds at the back of the system as it takes the rain away with it to the east.

Red sky in the morning, sailor's warning: as the rising sun in the east lights up approaching clouds in the west, the frontal system is on the way.

Beaufort Wind Scale

	Force	Speed	Description	Observations
Good beginners' breeze	0	0–1 knots	Calm	Sea like a mirror. Smoke rises vertically.
	1	1–3 knots	Light air	Ripples have appearance of scales on water. Smoke drift and flags indicate direction.
	2	4–6 knots	Light breeze	Small wavelets with glassy crests. Wind can be felt on the face. Flags and wind vanes also indicate direction.
	3	7–10 knots	Gentle breeze	Large wavelets. Crests begin to break, producing scattered white horses. Leaves and branches begin to move. Ideal conditions to learn to sail. Limit of wind for beginners.
Advanced sailing	4	11–16 knots	Moderate breeze	Small waves, becoming larger; frequent white horses. Dinghies require more work to keep balanced.
	5	17–21 knots	Fresh winds	Moderate waves, take a more pronounced shape with regular white horses formed from spray. Chance of capsize. Small trees sway in wind and flags fly horizontally.
	6	22–27 knots	Strong winds	Large waves with white foam crests and spray are extensive. Limit of safety for dinghies. Large trees sway and wind whistles.

Frontal Systems and Weather Maps

Most weather in Europe is caused by the passage of frontal systems, or depressions, or low pressure systems over the continent. A basic understanding of these and regular looks at the associated synoptic chart (the weather map) will soon allow a reasonable level of forecasting ability to be attained.

The basic source of weather is the interaction between different air masses. Broadly speaking there are four types of air mass:

Polar air masses: cold and dry air from the polar regions

Tropical air masses: warm, wet air from the tropical ocean areas

Maritime air masses: relatively wet air coming from non-tropical ocean areas

Continental air masses: relatively dry air coming from large land masses

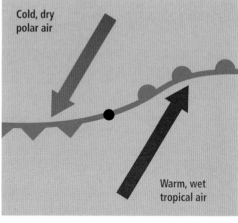

Figure 2

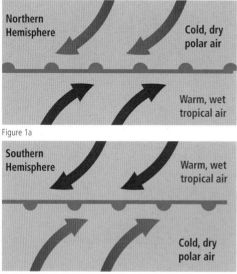

Figure 1a

Figure 1b

The frontal systems that cause most European weather are caused by the interaction of cold dry polar air coming from the Arctic and the warm wet air coming from the Atlantic.

An eddy forms (just like those seen in water running by a pontoon), and the system may start to rotate (anticlockwise in the Northern Hemisphere, (Fig 1a) clockwise in the Southern (Fig 1b).

This is where two major features are formed – the warm and cold fronts. These are quite simply the front of the relatively warm and wet and relatively cold and dry air masses (Fig 2). A domestic example is the bathroom in the morning. Hot, moisture laden air meets a cold, dry mirror, and condensation immediately forms. Warm and cold fronts are much larger versions of that, but are fundamentally down to the meeting of two different air masses. The section of air between the two fronts is the relatively warm and wet air mass, known as the warm sector.

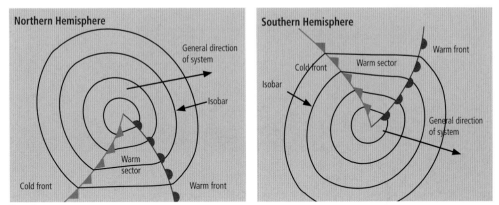

Figure 3

With the frontal system fully developed and usually moving to the north east or east, there is a complete circulation around the centre of the low, just as in little whirlpools on the edge of a fast flowing stream. This can be seen in terms of a pressure map, otherwise known as a synoptic chart. (Fig 3)

Here, the warm and cold fronts are represented, and the shape of the system as a whole is shown by the isobars, or lines of equal pressure. These isobars are the first forecasting tool, as the wind direction is generally about 10 to 15 degrees off the line of the isobar, offset inwards towards the centre of the low. Wind strength is directly related to the spacing between the isobars (the pressure gradient. Fig 4). The closer the isobars, the more the pressure gradient, and therefore the stronger the wind. Once the wind direction and strength has been looked at, the weather is next. This is driven by what is happening in the air above the dinghy.

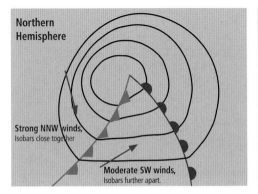

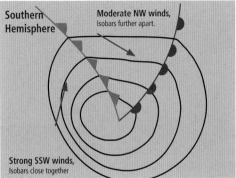

Figure 4

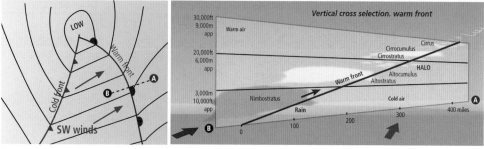

Figure 5

As the front goes over, the rain will reach its maximum, and the visibility will drop. Once the front has passed, the rain will ease up, and the visibility will improve, but not back to how it was before the front, as the warm sector air mass is relatively warm and wet and so will hold more moisture and not be as clear. (Fig 5)

The cloud cover will be mostly stratus or nimbostratus, and there may be fairly steady rain. The wind will have veered, and will be reasonably constant in strength and direction.

The cold front is a very different animal to the warm front. As the air mass is cold and dry, it cannot climb up and over the warm sector air mass, so all the interaction between the two air masses happens in almost the same vertical plane, potentially allowing the formation of massive cumulonimbus clouds. (Fig 6)

The conditions under the front are potentially dangerous, with unpredictable squalls coming off the edges of the cumulonimbus clouds, heavy rain or hail and electrical storms all possible. As a result of all this, visibility may be very poor.

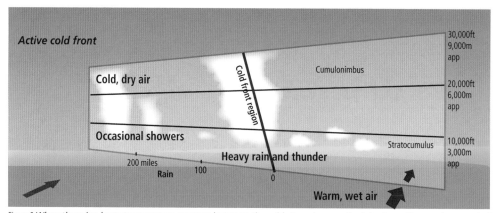

Figure 6 *When there is a large temperature contrast between the cold air and warm air, violent weather can be expected along the cold front, with rain squalls and perhaps hail and thunder.*

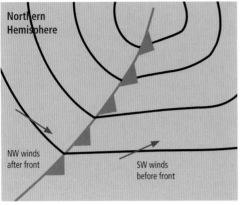

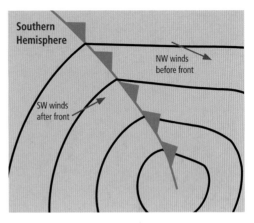

Figure 7

After the cold front has passed, however, the wind will veer again, the skies will clear almost immediately, and as the air is now part of the cold, dry mass, the visibility will be excellent and there may be some scenic cumulus clouds if any. (Fig 7)

As the whole system becomes more mature the cold front will start to catch up with the warm front, very much like a zipper being done up. This forms an occluded front and results in what's left of the warm sector being pushed up above the preceding and following cold air masses which now join up. (Fig 8)

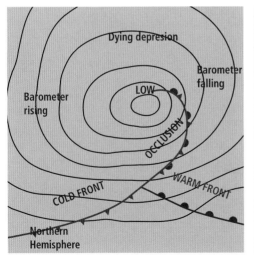

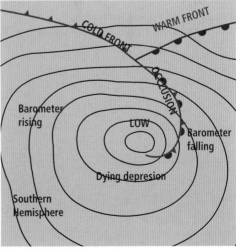

Figure 8 a

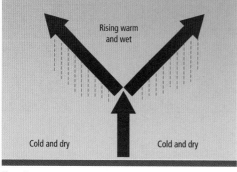

Figure 9

As all this warm wet air is lifted, it cools, causing moisture to come out of the air in the form of a persistent, miserable drizzle and low level cloud. (Fig 9) As this is towards the end of the frontal system's life it's normally not very energetic.

High Pressure Systems and their Interaction with Low Pressure Systems

High pressure systems are generally found over large ocean masses, for example the North Atlantic or Azores High. They are not as mobile as low pressure systems, and are also generally composed of just one air mass, and so do not have the fronts associated with a low. In the Northern Hemisphere they rotate clockwise (anticlockwise in the Southern Hemisphere) and are represented by isobars as with low pressure systems.

The same rules apply for wind strength and direction as before – the direction of the isobars are broadly speaking the direction of the wind around the high, with the wind offset by 10 to 15 degrees away from the centre of it. The wind strength is governed by the spacing in between the isobars, the pressure gradient.

High pressure systems can bring balmy weather, and in European waters over summer this is often the case, with the centre of a high sitting over northern France bringing light and variable winds to most of the European continent.

However, if a relatively static high acts as a buffer for a strong low (Fig 10), then very large pressure gradients can occur between the

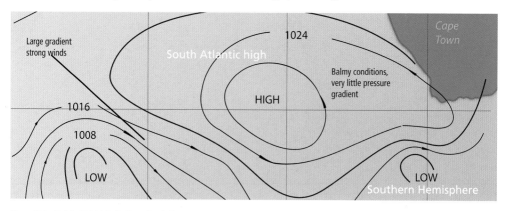

Figure 10 South Atlantic high in Southern Hemisphere.

systems, causing very strong winds, as illustrated, for the Southern Hemisphere above.

Fog

Fog is basically sea level cloud, and is caused in two ways; radiation or land fog. This occurs either when there is not much gradient wind, there is a change in sea temperature or a drop in wind speed. A high pressure system overhead is an ideal circumstance.

During the day the air will heat up over the shore and over the sea, and moisture will be taken in by the air as it heats up. Fig 11) As soon as the sun goes down, the air will cool and start to release this moisture in the form of fog. It will collect in low lying areas, e.g. harbours and river valleys, and will occasionally spill out up to two or three miles from land. When the sun rises, the air will heat up again, the moisture will go back into suspension, and the fog will clear – this is what is meant by the sun "burning off" the fog. So, if at breakfast there is no visibility and little wind, then by about 11:00 the fog will have gone and sailing will be possible (depending on the wind).

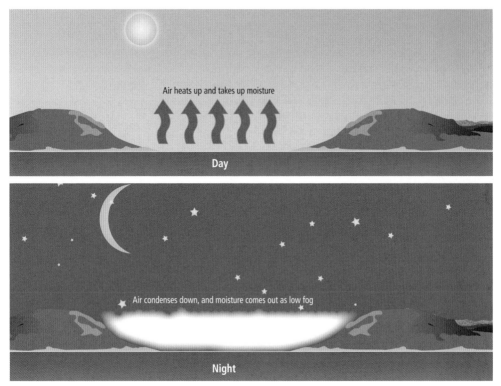

Air heats up and takes up moisture

Day

Air condenses down, and moisture comes out as low fog

Night

Figure 11

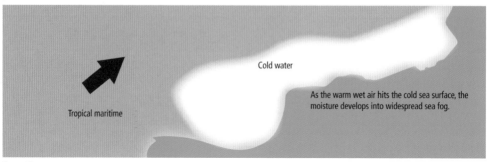

Cold water

As the warm wet air hits the cold sea surface, the moisture develops into widespread sea fog.

Tropical maritime

Figure 12

After the sun goes down, the air cools, releasing moisture, which develops into night fog. (Fig 12)

Advection, or Sea Fog

This is caused by relatively warm wet air blowing over cold water. The cold sea surface cools the surface air, causing the moisture to come out of suspension as fog. This occurs mostly in the spring, when water temperature is coldest after winter and the tropical maritime air masses are being brought in from warmer latitudes. (Fig 13)

This fog is more difficult to shift. An increase in wind speed just brings in more moisture, and sea fog will still be there up to a Force 7. Because new moisture is being brought in constantly, the sun cannot heat up the air sufficiently. The only way for sea fog to dissipate is for another air mass, either a polar maritime (cold and relatively dry) or a continental (dry and warm) air to come in. This requires a change in the wind direction. (Fig 13)

Visibility	
Good	More than 5 miles (9.25km)
Moderate	2-5 miles (3.7-9.25km)
Poor	0.5-2 miles (1-3.7km)
Fog	Less than 0.5mile (1km)

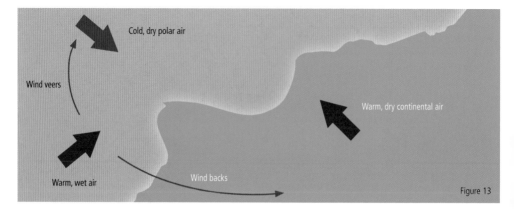

Cold, dry polar air

Wind veers

Warm, dry continental air

Warm, wet air

Wind backs

Figure 13

Weather terms

Barometric tendency – The rise or fall of the barometer at three-hour intervals, giving an early indication to a change in the weather.

Cyclonic – Term often used in shipping forecasts when a low is tracking through a sea area and wind shifts are difficult to predict.

Depressions – Rotating frontal systems.

Front – The front edge of a relatively warm, wet air mass (for a warm front) or a relatively cold, dry air mass (for a cold front).

Gradient wind – The wind caused by pressure difference. Wind flowing from high and low pressure, which is affected by the rotation of the earth's surface, causing it to blow around high and low pressure systems. The closer the isobars, the stronger the wind.

Gusts – Parcels of fast-moving air sucked down by rising thermal currents, which last for several minutes. Strong gusts occur when the descending upper wind is reinforced by downdraughts on the surface generated by heavy rain and thunderstorms.

Line squall – A cold front often marked by a line of low black cloud, which brings with it a sharp rise in wind speed and direction for a short term.

Mistral – Localized strong to gale force wind. This particular wind refers to the predictable slope wind that blows down the Rhône Valley and extends out across the Rhône delta into the Gulf of Lions. Forecasters can usually predict its passage to within minutes. This phenomen occurs in many parts of the world. It is known as the Meltemi in the Aegean Sea, Tramontana or Garigliano on the west coast of Italy and northern Corsica, and the Hamatan off West Africa.

Troughs – Frontal troughs are easily recognizable as a line of changing weather. Non-frontal troughs are harder to pick up, as the air mass does not change discernibly as the front passes through. However, the pressure falls ahead and rises behind and winds back ahead and veer behind. Troughs often follow a cold front and rotate around a depression like the spokes of a wheel.

Veering and backing winds – A veering wind changes direction in a clockwise direction and a backing wind moves anticlockwise.

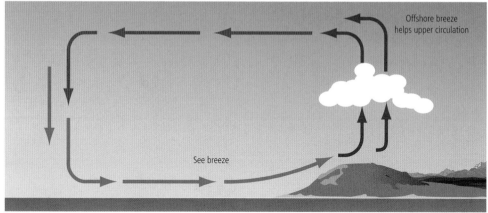

Offshore breeze helps upper circulation

See breeze

Figure 14

Sea Breezes

Sea breezes are a dinghy sailor's lifeline on hot, balmy summer days. They are caused by the difference in warming characteristics between land and sea. (Fig 14)

The land will heat up faster than the sea, and so the air above the land will heat up faster than that above the sea. This makes it expand and rise up. As it expands upwards, it also expands outwards, and pushes out to sea. As there is now physically less air over the land and more air over the sea, a localised

low pressure is formed over the land, and a localised high pressure formed over the sea, which causes a sea level breeze- the sea breeze- to blow from the sea towards the shore.

As the afternoon wears on, the continual rising of moisture laden air above the land will cause cumulus clouds to form along the coast. Also, if there is a slight offshore high level wind, this helps the development of the sea breeze.

Wind Shadows and Funnelling

These two effects are entirely local, and are a function of large obstructions around and through which the wind has to pass.

Any tall object, such as a moored cargo ship or a large headland, will have a wind shadow on its leeward side (Fig 15). As an approximate rule of thumb the wind shadow of an obstruction will be approximately six times its height. By looking for ripples on the water it is often possible to see where the wind shadow finishes, and plan the route accordingly.

Tips

❶ Know your limitations and always sail in company

❷ Always get a forecast for the time you intend to sail plus a bit.

❸ Always tell someone where you are going and when you intend to be back.

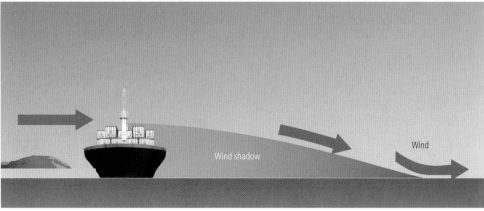

Figure 15

When sailing near river valleys or in harbours with many tall buildings nearby, there will be alleys between these obstructions where the wind will be funnelled, causing very sudden and local areas of increased and possibly shifted wind (Fig16). Again, by keeping an eye open for the change in surface ripples caused by a change in wind characteristics, some warning can be had. Another sign is boats in front of you suddenly heeling heavily while sailing upwind, or broaching out of control when sailing downwind.

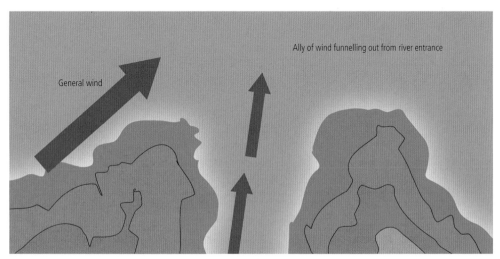

Figure 16

First sail

Balance, sail, trim

If you have not sailed before, we strongly recommend having an instructor onboard to show you the basics. Choose a day when the winds are moderate and the tidal stream is slack. Start on a beam reach (90° to the wind) with sheets eased halfway out and get the feel of the boat.

The controls

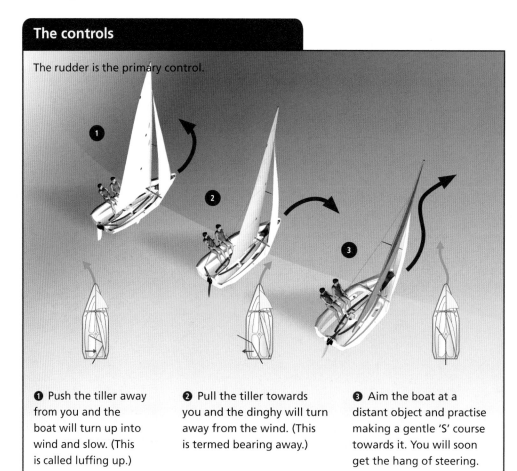

The rudder is the primary control.

❶ Push the tiller away from you and the boat will turn up into wind and slow. (This is called luffing up.)

❷ Pull the tiller towards you and the dinghy will turn away from the wind. (This is termed bearing away.)

❸ Aim the boat at a distant object and practise making a gentle 'S' course towards it. You will soon get the hang of steering.

Balance

It's the crew's job to balance the boat as well as trim the jib.

If the wind is moderate, they will invariably need to sit on the side deck alongside the helm to keep the boat flat. If it heels more, then both helm and crew will need to hook their feet under the toe straps and lean out to counter the force of wind on the sails.

If the wind drops, then the crew needs to come inboard and sit on the central thwart to keep the boat on an even keel.

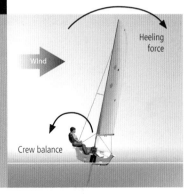

Wind

Heeling force

Crew balance

Stopping
Release the sheets and let the sails right out so they flap.

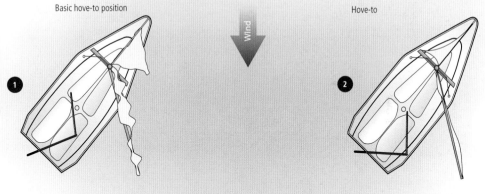

Basic hove-to position

Wind

Hove-to

❶ **1**

❷ **2**

❶ Basic hove-to. As the dinghy slows, the helm steers the bows towards the wind and releases the mainsheet until the sails are empty of wind. Then centre the rudder.

❷ To lie hove-to for a longer period, with the boat stable, stopped and quiet, simply pull the jib in hard on the windward side and cleat the sheet and push the rudder hard over to counter the rotating force of the jib. The boat will now stay balanced at a close reach angle to the wind on its own.

To start again, the crew releases the jib and sheets it in on the opposite side. Helm bears away to resume their course and trims mainsail to suit.

Sail trim

The sails can also have a turning effect on the boat. Bring the dinghy back into a basic hove-to position, then pull in on the mainsail alone. The dinghy will turn towards the wind.

Return to the basic hove-to position and then pull in the jib alone. The dinghy will turn away from the wind.

Keeping the jib and mainsail sheeted in balance with each other lessens the weight on the helm and the effort needed to steer the boat.

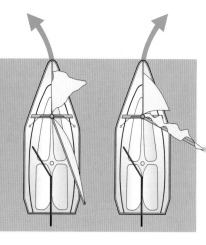

From reach to sailing close-hauled

❺ Crew move in and out to balance the boat.

❹ Helm maintains close-hauled course, testing how close to the wind to sail by pointing up until the jib luff just starts to flutter and windward tell-tale is lifting.

No-go zone

Wind

❸ With sails sheeted in hard, helm watches for the jib luff to start fluttering then bears away slightly until jib sets and luff tell-tales are flying parallel.

❶ Helm pushes tiller away to head the boat closer to the wind. Crew push the centreboard fully down.

❷ Helm and crew pull in the sheets to stop the sails from flapping.

Going about
Turning through 180° from one beam reach angle to the other.

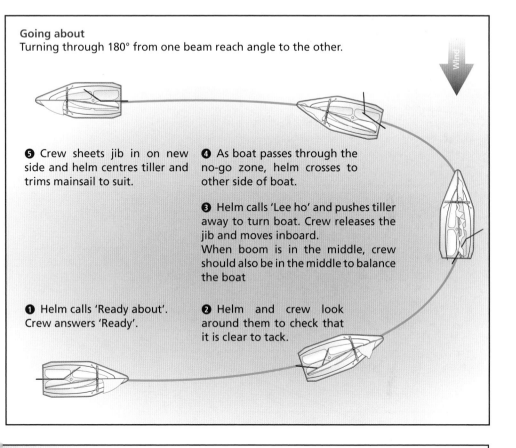

5 Crew sheets jib in on new side and helm centres tiller and trims mainsail to suit.

4 As boat passes through the no-go zone, helm crosses to other side of boat.

3 Helm calls 'Lee ho' and pushes tiller away to turn boat. Crew releases the jib and moves inboard.
When boom is in the middle, crew should also be in the middle to balance the boat

1 Helm calls 'Ready about'. Crew answers 'Ready'.

2 Helm and crew look around them to check that it is clear to tack.

Sailing closer to the wind requires adjustment of the sails, centreboard and possibly crew weight. As the helm pushes the tiller over to turn the bows progressively closer to the wind:

- Crew puts centreboard right down to minimize leeway.

- Mainsail and jib start to flap (stall) and are progressively pulled in until sheets are hard in and boat is sailing at about 45° to the wind.
- Depending on the wind strength, crew hike outboard to balance the boat and counter the greater heeling effect on the rig.

No-go zone

This is when the boat is pointing directly into wind. The boat will come to a halt, and without steerage way, the rudder will have no effect. There is also the danger of the boom thrashing about in the wind and hitting you on the head, so beware. This is the one point of sail to be avoided.

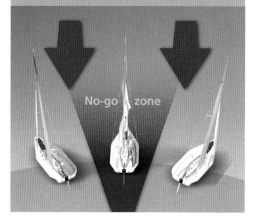

To break out, the crew pushes the boom out on the leeward side so that the mainsail is back-winded and helm pushes the rudder away. The boat will start moving backwards in an arc. As the bows swing round away from the wind, the crew releases the boom and sheets the jib on the leeward side, As the sails fill, helm pulls the tiller over to get the boat on a set course and sheets in the mainsail to suit.

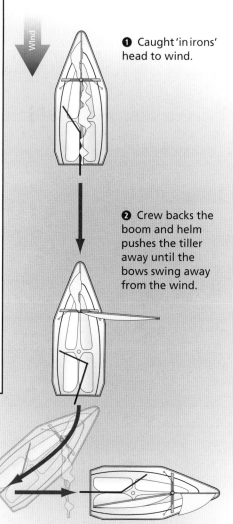

❶ Caught 'in irons' head to wind.

❷ Crew backs the boom and helm pushes the tiller away until the bows swing away from the wind.

❸ Crew sheets in the jib. Helm centres tiller and trims main to suit new course.

Lifting daggerboard configuration

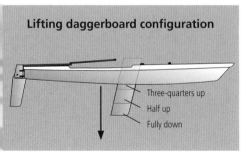

Three-quarters up
Half up
Fully down

Hinged centreboard configuration

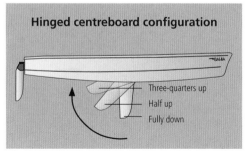

Three-quarters up
Half up
Fully down

Centreboard/daggerboard

The position of the centreboard (and to a lesser extent the daggerboard in boats like the Laser single-hander) will affect the relationship between the boat's centre of effort and centre of lateral resistance and will affect the boat's balance as well as leeway. (see page 16)

When sailing to windward (about 45° to the wind) with sails pulled in tight, the centreboard has to be right down to minimize the strong sideways force (termed leeway) from the rig. Try pulling the board up while sailing to windward and you will appreciate how effective it is in reducing sideways drift. The boat will start 'crabbing' sideways immediately, even though it is still pointing in the same direction.

When reaching, there is less sideways pressure on the sails, so the board can be raised progressively the further the boat is pointed away from the wind until sailing dead downwind when there is no leeway effect at all. It is a good idea to keep a small amount of board down to help maintain direction.

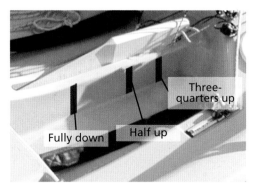

Three-quarters up

Fully down   Half up

Tacking

Tacking with a centre mainsheet boat

The first task is to prepare the boat and crew:

- Check that main and jib sheets are free to run.

- Look around to check that you are clear of other boats to windward.

- Helm maintains a grip on tiller extension with one hand and the mainsheet with in the other.

- Helm warns crew by calling 'Ready about'.

- Crew answers 'Ready' and uncleats jib sheet.

- Helm pushes tiller away without changing hands and calls out 'Lee ho'.

- As boat heads up into wind, crew moves inboard.

- Helm continues to steer boat up into wind without changing hands.

- As the boat turns through the wind, crew releases the jib sheet, and helm and crew move into the centre of the boat, ducking under the boom.

- Helm and crew move across to new windward side, helm now steering with the tiller hand behind his back and mainsheet in his opposite hand. He straightens the tiller as sails fill on the opposite tack.

- Helm now changes hands on tiller extension and sheet.

- Helm and crew adjust sails to match the wind angle on new course and balance the boat.

4 Helm sits on the windward side deck, still holding the tiller extension with his right hand, now behind his back, while continuing to hold the mainsheet with his left hand.

3 As boat turns through the eye of the wind, helm ducks under the boom and crosses to the other side while facing forward, leading with their back foot first. Crew starts to pull in the jib sheet on other side.

2 Helm calls 'Lee ho' and pushes tiller away to point the boat up into wind. Crew releases the jib sheet and comes inboard to balance the boat.

5 Helm now grasps the tiller extension with his left hand, and swaps the mainsheet to his right hand. Crew sheets the jib in hard and prepares to climb up onto starboard side deck to balance the boat.

6 Helm and crew trims the mainsheet to suit. Crew balances the boat. Helm centres the rudder onto the new tack.

Wind

5

4

3

2

1

1 Helm checks that it is clear to tack. Helm warns crew with call 'Ready about' and uncleats mainsheet. Crew answers 'Ready' and uncleats jib sheet.

Tacking with an aft mainsheet boat

- Check that main and jib sheets are free to run.

- Look around to check that you are clear of other boats to windward.

- Change hands on the tiller extension.

- Push the tiller away while facing the back of th boat.

- As boat heads up into wind, move inboard, ducking under boom.

- Helm moves across to new windward side, extends tiller arm and straightens rudder as sail fills on the opposite tack.

- Helm and crew adjust sails to match the wind angle on new course and balance the boat.

6 Crew gives a final tug on the jib sheet and continues to balance the boat while keeping a watch for obstacles and potential collision situations.

Wind

5 Boat now on starboard tack. Helm centres the tiller to maintain this course and sheets in the mainsail to suit.

4 Helm turns to sit on the windward side deck, keeping the rudder over as the boat continues to turn through the eye of the wind. Crew sheets in the jib and prepares to sit up on the side deck if necessary.

2 Helm calls 'Lee ho' and transfers the mainsheet to his aft hand and the tiller extension to his forward hand before pushing tiller away to point the boat up into wind. Crew releases the jib sheet and comes inboard to balance the boat.

3 Helm steps across the boat facing aft and ducks under the boom, moving his forward foot across first. Crew pulls the jib round on the opposite side while continuing to balance the boat.

1 Helm checks that it is clear to tack. Helm warns crew with call 'Ready about' and uncleats mainsheet. Crew answers 'Ready' and uncleats jib sheet.

Trim

The dynamics wind and water have on a boat can alter when sailing at different angles to the wind. The crew can take advantage of of this by moving their weight fore and aft to keep the edge of the transom just kissing the surface, and not dragging in the water.

- Sailing close-hauled, crew weight should be centred forward, close to the shrouds.
- In light airs, you also sit right forward to lift the transom out the the water and reduce wetted area of the hull.
- Always sit as far far forward as possible, moving weight back only when the bows start to dig in.
- A flat boat is a fast boat.

Remember the five essentials to safe sailing

✓ Maintain good balance, keeping the dinghy almost vertical.

✓ Trim the boat to keep the transom from dragging in the water.

✓ Adjust the centreboard for each point of sailing.

✓ Keep sails trimmed to the wind direction or course – and reef when necessary.

✓ Set a course to avoid other boats and hazards.

Sailing downwind

The training run is where the wind is blowing over the quarter the sails are out and the jib is empty because it is shielded from the wind by the mainsail.

- Practise turning from a beam reach, through a broad reach to the training run and back to sailing close-hauled.
- When sailing dead downwind you can set the jib on the windward side, either by attaching a whisker pole between mast and clew of the sail, or for the helm to hold the jib out with his forward hand.
- Sailing by the lee with the wind crossing the leeward aft quarter should be avoided because the wind can get behind the mainsail, forcing it to swing across in a crash gybe.

The training run is the most efficient point of sailing downwind because the angle encourages airflow across the sails.

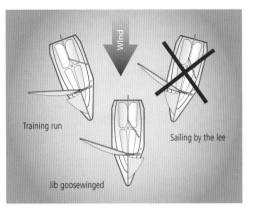

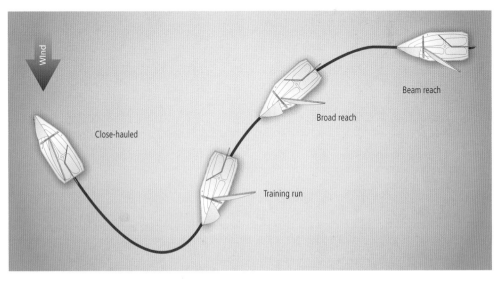

Gybing

Gybing a centre -mainsheet boat

Gybing takes the the back of the boat through the wind.

- Start from a training run and check to leeward that there are no other boats or hazards in the vicinity.

- Helm warns the crew by calling 'Ready to gybe'. Crew answers 'Yes'

- Helm calls 'Gybe ho' and pulls the tiller towards them while facing forward in the boat.

- As the boom starts to come across, the tiller is centred. Remember to duck!

- Helm and crew swap sides in the boat.

- Helm steers with hand behind back.

- Once on the weather side, helm changes tiller hand.

- Crew trims jib on new side and balances the boat.

❹ As the mainsail fills on the starboard side, the crew moves to balance the boat and sheets the jib. Helm moves across to the sidedeck and swaps hands on the tiller extension and mainsheet.

❸ As the stern passes through the eye of the wind, the crew helps the boom across by pulling on the kicking strap/vang or centre-mainsheet. Helm centres the rudder and crosses the boat facing forward. Helm and crew keep their heads down as the boom swings across.

❷ Helm bears away while facing forward and rotates the tiller extension to the leeward side. Crew picks up the sheet on the opposite side and moves into the centre of the boat.

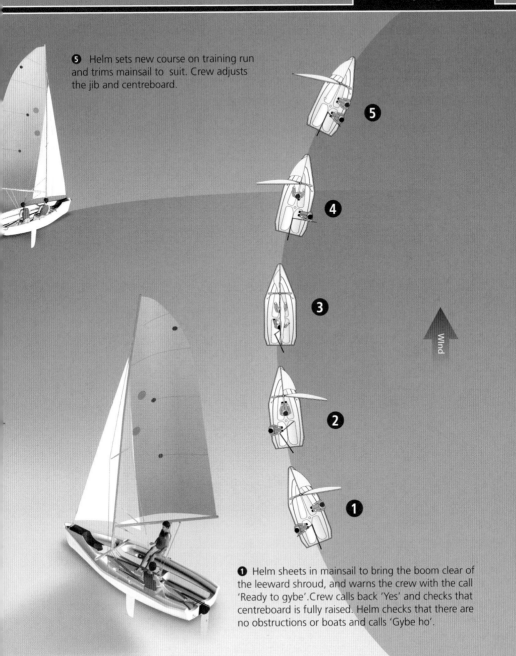

Gybing

5 Helm sets new course on training run and trims mainsail to suit. Crew adjusts the jib and centreboard.

Wind

1 Helm sheets in mainsail to bring the boom clear of the leeward shroud, and warns the crew with the call 'Ready to gybe'. Crew calls back 'Yes' and checks that centreboard is fully raised. Helm checks that there are no obstructions or boats and calls 'Gybe ho'.

Dinghy Sailing | 105

Gybing an aft-mainsheet boat

Gybing an older fashioned dinghy with an aft-mainsheet system attached to the transom, requires a different technique on the part of the helm, to gybing a boat with a centre-mainsheet.

The main difference is that the helm faces aft during the manoeuvre, and changes hands on the tiller and mainsheet before the boom swings across.

■ Start from a training run and check to leeward that there are no other boats or hazards in the vicinity.

■ Helm warns the crew by calling 'Ready to gybe'. Crew answers 'Yes'

■ Helm swaps hands on tiller and mainsheet.

■ Helm calls 'Gybe ho' and pulls the tiller towards them.

■ As the boom starts to come across, the tiller is centred. Remember to duck!

■ Helm and crew swap sides in the boat. Helm faces aft, leading with his forward leg.

■ Once on the weather side, helm steers on new course and sets mainsail to suit.

■ Crew trims jib on new side and balances the boat.

❹ As the mainsail fills on the starboard gybe, the crew moves to balance the boat and sheet the jib. Helm moves across to the sidedeck.

❸ As the stern passes through the eye of the wind, the crew helps the boom across by pulling on the kicking strap. Helm centres the rudder and crosses the boat facing aft. Helm and crew keep their heads down as the boom swings across.

❷ Helm turns the rudder to windward to bear away and turning to face aft, swaps hands on the tiller extension and mainsheet. Crew picks up the sheet on the opposite side and moves into the centre of the boat.

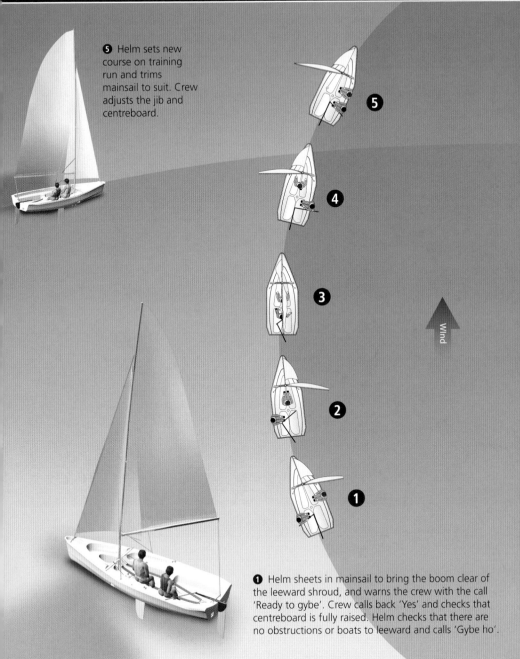

5 Helm sets new course on training run and trims mainsail to suit. Crew adjusts the jib and centreboard.

Wind

1 Helm sheets in mainsail to bring the boom clear of the leeward shroud, and warns the crew with the call 'Ready to gybe'. Crew calls back 'Yes' and checks that centreboard is fully raised. Helm checks that there are no obstructions or boats to leeward and calls 'Gybe ho'.

Capsize and recovery

Capsize drill

It is a good idea to practise this on a calm day. Capsizing is a common enough occurrence when racing dinghies. It is certainly something to try and avoid, but not fear. When you know the drill, the worst that can happen – is you get wet!

The scoop method of recovery

This method 'scoops' the crew back into the boat as it is righted. Crew pushes the centreboard/daggerboard right down.

❶ Helm (or heaviest person) swims round the stern and prepares to climb up on the centreboard.

❹ Crew floats facing forward inside the hull holding onto the toe strap or thwart.

❺ Helm allows the boat to turn up into wind before exerting their weight on the jib sheet to haul the boat upright. If helm pulls the boat upright before it is facing into wind, the mainsail is likely to fill and capsize the dinghy the other way.

❷ Crew throws the end of the 'upper' jib sheet over the gunwale for helm to use as a hauling line.

❸ Helm grabs the jib sheet, climbs on the centreboard and prepares to lean back on the sheet.

❻ As the boat comes upright, crew scrambles aboard, balances the boat and releases the jib sheet.

❼ Helm can either climb over the windward gunwale as the boat comes upright, or is helped aboard by crew once the dinghy is stable. Crew then gather themselves together and reach off on the fastest point of sailing to drain the cockpit of water before resuming their course.

Recovery from full inversion

❶ If your dinghy inverts, helm and crew must work together to right the boat. Crew swims round to retrieve the jib sheet or hauling line and throws it over the hull.

❷ Helm climbs on the hull and pulls the centreboard out as crew swims back round to assist righting.

❹ Allow the boat to turn up into wind before exerting weight on the jib sheet to haul the boat upright.

❺ As boat comes upright, helm climbs back in to release sheets and lines and balance the boat.

3 Crew climbs up alongside helm and together they pull the boat back on its side.

6 NEVER climb in over the stern. If the sails fill, the boat will take off - dragging you behind it!

TIP

The golden rule is to always keep one hand on the boat.

Trapped under a sail

Don't panic. Simply push the sail up off the water to create an air pocket and swim out.

Trapped under the boat

Again, don't panic. Simply pull yourself to one side of the boat, shake yourself free of any ropes, and pull yourself out under the gunwale.

Returning to shore

Windward shoreline

Plan your windward course back to the beach, bank or slipway and make sure the crew fully understands – because it is their job to jump out and hold the boat.

- After the final tack, helm raises the rudder or releases the elasticated downhaul.

- Helm turns the boat head to wind and crew raises the centreboard.
- As boat reaches the shallows, crew jumps out just aft of the windward shroud and holds the bows into wind.
- Put the boat on it trolley and pull up the beach before lowering sails.

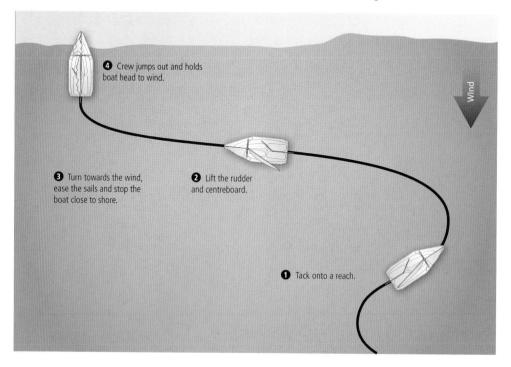

④ Crew jumps out and holds boat head to wind.

Wind

③ Turn towards the wind, ease the sails and stop the boat close to shore.

② Lift the rudder and centreboard.

① Tack onto a reach.

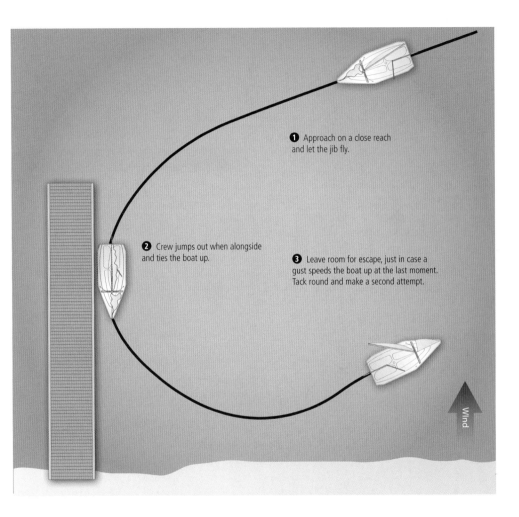

1 Approach on a close reach and let the jib fly.

2 Crew jumps out when alongside and ties the boat up.

3 Leave room for escape, just in case a gust speeds the boat up at the last moment. Tack round and make a second attempt.

Wind

Alongside a pontoon

The key is to make your approach slowly by letting out the sails in good time – and plan an escape route just in case you don't!

- Approach on a close reach.
- Release the sails to slow the boat down in good time.
- Turn head to wind and come alongside.
- Crew has the painter (bow rope) ready and keeps fingers clear of the gunwale.
- When the boat stops, crew disembarks to tie the boat up and helm lowers the sails.
- If you overshoot, use the boat speed to tack round and make the attempt again.

Lee shoreline

If the weather is poor, and you are inexperienced, avoid beaching on a lee shore. Find somewhere safer to land. Beginners should only attempt this in calm weather.

If conditions allow, the cautious way is to:

- Turn up into wind some way offshore, clear of the breaking waves, and take the mainsail down.
- Turn back downwind under jib alone.
- At the last moment helm raises the rudder or releases the elasticated downhaul.
- As the boat reaches shallow enough water, for the crew to stand, they jump out and hold the boat.

- If the waters are calm, the boat can be put on its trolley. If not, then drag the boat up clear of the water, and turn it into wind, then lower the sails.

TIP

Practise in clear water away from the area you want to stop. Point the boat in the direction you must stop and let all the sails out. If the mainsail flaps, you can keep it up. If it fills, then take it down before making your final approach.

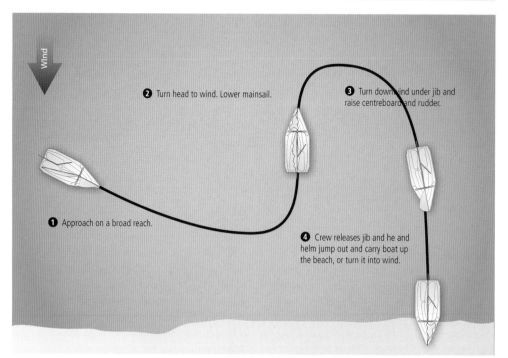

Wind

❷ Turn head to wind. Lower mainsail.

❸ Turn downwind under jib and raise centreboard and rudder.

❶ Approach on a broad reach.

❹ Crew releases jib and he and helm jump out and carry boat up the beach, or turn it into wind.

When the pontoon is broadside to the wind:

- Turn up into wind some way offshore, and take the mainsail down.
- Turn back downwind under jib alone.
- As helm turns to approach the pontoon, crew releases the jib sheet.
- Allow the boat to drift in on the wind.
- Crew has the painter (bow rope) ready and keeps fingers clear of the gunwale.
- When the boat stops, crew disembarks to tie the boat up and helms lowers the jib.

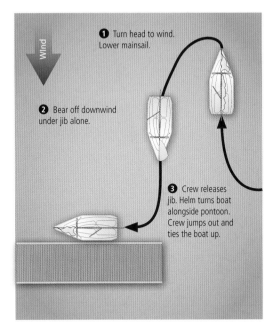

❶ Turn head to wind. Lower mainsail.

Wind

❷ Bear off downwind under jib alone.

❸ Crew releases jib. Helm turns boat alongside pontoon. Crew jumps out and ties the boat up.

Advanced sailing

Once you have mastered the basics of sailing, the best way to improve your technique and learn the finer points is to join a club and start racing. Either buy a boat that the club has already fostered or better still, learn by crewing for others and choose a boat later with the benefit of experience, when you know which class will give you the most fun and competition.

Now it is time to master the art of maximizing performance, and perhaps graduating to a more exciting boat like the Laser Vago or Dart 16X catamaran.

Trapezing

The key to trapezing is a comfortable harness. Many experienced sailors prefer the 'nappy' harness for its comfort and ease of use, but this design does not provide the lumber support provided by the traditional full harness. Spend time adjusting the straps so that the hook is positioned low down and tight around your abdomen, and shoulder straps support your back.

The strapping may feel too tight when you are walking around the dinghy pen, but will be a reassuringly snug fit when you are suspended out on the wire, spreading your weight evenly across the lower body and back.

Next, adjust the length of the trapeze wires so that you can hook on while out on the gunwale and the handle is at a comfortable

❶ *Setting up the trapeze eye with an elastic retaining cord linked to the eye on the opposite side.*

❷ *Tie a loop into the end of the shock cord. Pass this though the eye*

❸ *Pass the loop over the back of the eye and pull tight, and repeat on the oppose side.*

height for you to support your upper body weight with one hand as you push out.

Practise makes perfect. Go out on a relatively calm day when the sails and the helm, sitting on the lee side, will counter- balance your weight out on the wire. Start by getting out onto the trapeze and back into the boat and continue the exercise on one tack until your movements are smooth and confidence builds. Then practise tacking, swinging in, unhooking and moving across the boat while tacking the jib and swinging back out on the opposite side.

Trapezing

- Check out the harness and trapeze connections before going afloat.

- Hold the jib sheet in your forward hand and hook the trapeze to the harness with the other. Slide out over the gunwale until the wire takes your weight.

- Push yourself out with your front foot at right angles to the boat, and balance yourself using your aft arm, and feet a body width apart on the gunwale.

- Balance your weight against the heeling forces of the sails by bending your aft leg first to bring your weight inboard during the lulls, and stretching right out in the gusts. Always keep the jib or spinnaker sheet in your forward hand ready to release should the dinghy become overpowered.

■ When beating to windward, centre your weight just behind the shrouds.

■ When reaching or running, you should be constantly moving your body back and forward one or two steps along the gunwale to trim the boat and promote planing.

■ Be prepared to resist the sudden pull forward, should the bows hit a wave, by keeping the front knee 'locked'. Some dinghies have foot straps fitted along the gunwale to tuck your aft foot under and stop yourself from being pulled forwards.

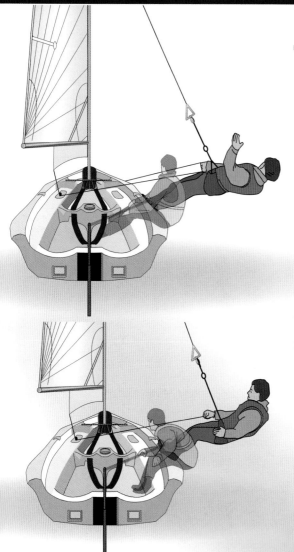

Tacking

Tacking with the trapeze

Tacking a trapeze boat requires greater agility and teamwork. It takes longer for the crew to come in off the trapeze and get back out on the other side, so the helm must learn to give plenty of warning and turn the boat slower through the wind.

❶ Helm calls 'Ready about' to warn crew of imminent tack and, whenever possible, times the manoeuvre to coincide with relatively flat water between waves.

❷ Helm heads up slightly to depower the boat and allow the crew to come in without having to let out lots of mainsheet - which would all have to be pulled in again on the opposite side and slow acceleration out of the tack.

❸ Helm calls 'lee ho' to signal the start of the tack and pushes the helm down to round the bows up into wind. Crew swings inboard, leading with their aft leg, and unhooks the trapeze.

7 Helm and crew settle in on new tack.

6 Crew swings out on the trapeze, pulling the jib in tight as he goes, while helm trims the mainsail to suit.

5 Helm and crew then cross to the opposite side of the boat, crew releasing the jib sheet as he comes inboard.

4 Helm eases mainsheet as the boat crosses head to wind.

Roll Tacking

This manoeuvre is well worth practising, because a well-executed roll tack will accelerate the boat onto the new tack and gain a boat length on rivals who fail to do it right.

The object of the exercise is to lean the boat to windward as the bows head into wind, then use crew weight to pull the boat back upright as soon as the sails fill on the opposite tack. This increases pressure on the sails and accelerates the boat forward. The advantage is particularly noticeable in light winds, but can still be effective up to force 4.

- Helm calls 'Ready about' to warn crew of imminent tack and, whenever possible, times the manoeuvre to coincide with relatively flat water between waves.
- Helm calls 'lee ho' to signal start of the tack and pushes the helm down to round the bows up into wind.

- At the same time, both helm and crew lean out momentarily to tilt the boat over to windward enough for the gunwale to kiss the water.
- Helm and crew then cross to the opposite side of the boat.
- As they do so, crew releases the jib sheet, but only after the bows have passed through the eye of the wind. This allows the jib to 'backwind' momentarily and helps to turn the bows round quicker, while minimizing excessive use of the rudder.

❶ As you prepare to tack, helm allows boat to heel. Crew goes to leeward side if necessary.

- Crew then lean out in unison to return the boat to an even keel just as the sails fill on the new tack, and the boat accelerates forward.
- Helm and crew then resume their normal positions to match the conditions and trim sails to suit.

4 As sails fill on new tack, helm and crew use their weight to pull the boat back upright.

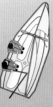

2 As the boat heads up into wind, both helm and crew lean the boat over to windward.

3 Helm and crew change sides.

Spinnaker handling

The symetric spinnaker adds considerable speed when broad reaching and sailing downwind. It takes practice and a good deal of coordination between helm and crew to use the sail effectively, so start out on a calm day to learn the ropes.

The spinnaker is symmetric in shape and should be set at 90° to the true wind direction. This is judged by the angle of the spinnaker pole. This can be varied by adjusting the windward sheet, which is known as the guy.

The second golden rule is to keep the clews level to the water in order to maintain the sail's designed shape. If the luff clew attached to the pole end is lower than the leech clew, the leading section of the spinnaker will be stretched too flat. If the luff clew is higher than that of the leech, then the spinnaker will be too open and collapse early. This is adjusted by raising or lowering the pole, usually by resetting the pole uphaul/downhaul line.

The only time this would vary is in very light and also strong winds. In light airs, a tighter luff will help the spinnaker to set. In a stronger breeze, a slacker luff opens the slot between spinnaker and jib and lessen the heeling force, so the pole end is set higher.

1 Clews set level.   **2** Pole set low for light airs.   **3** Pole set high for strong winds.

❶ Face boat downwind and hoist spinnaker with sheets attached.

❷ Haul spinnaker down into chute.

Stowing the spinnaker

Most modern dinghies have a spinnaker chute in the bow to launch and recover the spinnaker.

- The spinnaker should be set up in the chute before going afloat.
- Turn dinghy to head downwind.
- Attach the halyard and spinnaker sheets to the head and clews, and the downhaul line to the loop set within a strengthened patch in the centre of the sail.
- If conditions allow, hoist the spinnaker on the halyard ensuring that the spinnaker sheets remain free.
- Check that the sail is free of twists and then douse the spinnaker into the chute by pulling in the downhaul line until the head and clews are just showing in the mouth of the chute.
- The spinnaker is now ready for setting.

❸ Spinnaker head and clews just visible in mouth of chute, ready for hoisting.

If your dinghy does not have a spinnaker chute, then the sail is packed in a bag ready for a leeward hoist, usually on the port side of the mast. Check that the sail is packed without twists by running your hands down the luff or leech. The windward spinnaker sheet or guy is then run round the outside of the forestay and attached to the clew. The sheet must be run round the leeward shroud to ensure that the sail sets outside all the rigging.

Setting the spinnaker
- Helm bears away onto a broad reach or run and straddles the tiller between their knees.

❷ Crew connects spinnaker pole to mast and attaches uphaul. Helm takes sheet and guy in both hands and trims spinnaker.

❶ Helm straddles tiller and hoists spinnaker halyard. Crew connects spinnaker pole to windward sheet (guy).

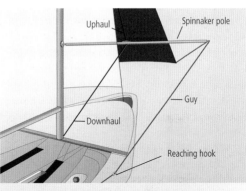

Uphaul

Spinnaker pole

Guy

Downhaul

Reaching hook

3 Helm cleats guy and passes sheet to crew. Crew puts windward sheet in reaching hook. Helm and crew resume positions and trim sails.

- Crew sets the windward guy in the outboard end of the pole before attaching the inboard end to the connection fitting on the front of the mast.
- Crew clips the guy in the reaching hook, then adjusts the pole angle at 90° to the wind before cleating it.
- Crew pulls in the spinnaker sheet only when the sail is fully hoisted. If the sheet is pulled in too early, then the spinnaker will set and make it difficult for the helm to pull the sail to the top of the mast.
- Crew resume position and course.
- Check pole height and angle and adjust if necessary.

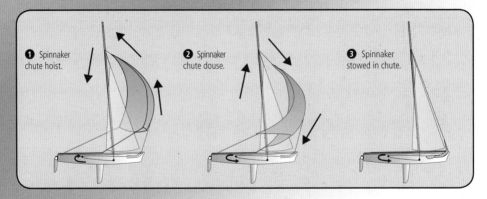

1 Spinnaker chute hoist.

2 Spinnaker chute douse.

3 Spinnaker stowed in chute.

Sheet adjustment

The spinnaker is very sensitive to wind strength and direction, and requires constant adjustment by the crew.

■ The key is to fine-trim the sheet so that the spinnaker luff tape is on the point of curling inwards. If the spinnaker is over-sheeted, the airflow across the sail will be choked and backwind the mainsail. If under-sheeted, the spinnaker will collapse.

■ Sailing with the spinnaker set in gusty conditions requires good coordination between helm and crew.

■ As the gust hits, crew eases the spinnaker sheet to allow the luff to curl.

■ The dinghy will then accelerate and the apparent wind will move forward.

■ Helm either bears away to compensate, or the crew sheets in on the spinnaker to stop it collapsing. In stronger conditions, it invariably requires a mix of both.

Luff on the point of curling inwards.

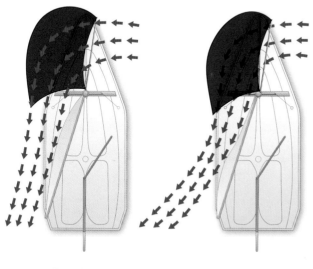

❶ Perfect set.

❷ Over-sheeted. Airflow choked in slot.

❸ Under-sheeted. Luff collapsed.

Gybing the spinnaker

1 Helm turns the boat onto a training run, so that the boat is flat and under control, straddles the tiller and takes both spinnaker sheets in left and right hands to keep the sail filled through the manoeuvre. Helm calls 'Standby to gybe'. Crew replies 'Yes' and releases the windward guy from the reaching hook. Helm calls 'Gybe-ho'.

3 Helm cleats off the guy and hands the leeward sheet to the crew. Helm and crew resume their normal positions and set sails for new course.

2 Crew pulls the boom across with the vang or mainsheet, and resets the mainsheet. Helm steers with the tiller between their knees and keeps the spinnaker flying by adjusting sheet and guy simultaneously. Crew disconnects pole and resets it on the new windward side.

Asymmetric spinnakers

Asymmetric spinnakers, like those on the Laser Bahia, simplify the setting and control considerably. This single luff sail is set on the end of a bowsprit, so there is no spinnaker pole or reaching hooks to worry about during a gybe and no concern about keeping the clews level.

Instead, the sail is controlled with double sheets just like a jib, though trim is the same as a spinnaker, with the need to keep the luff on the point of curling inwards. Even better, the bowsprit and spinnaker halyard/downhaul are interconnected so that the bowsprit extends and retracts automatically when the sail is hoisted and lowered. This is not the case with some older designs however, which have a separate control line for the bowsprit.

Gybing

Gybing is much easier too. As the stern turns through the wind, the crew sheet in the spinnaker by a metre to backwind the sail momentarily before letting the sheet fly. This encourages the asymmetric spinnaker to billow forward of the forestay and not rap itself around the jib. Once the gybe has been completed, the crew then sheet the sail in on the new side, just as if it was a jib.

❹ Helm sets new course and crew sheets spinnaker to suit.

Sailing downwind

Boats with asymmetric spinnakers are fastest on a broad reach. To take advantage of this, crews need to gybe downwind, zig-zagging down the course on a succession of broad reaches. In strong conditions, the sail can generate considerable lee helm, which is best countered by sailing the boat at a 10-15° angle of heel.

Performance dinghies with asymmetric spinnakers accelerate fast, so the helm will need to bear away in the gusts and be constantly aware of boats or obstructions to leeward.

Asymmetric rigs on modern dinghies like the Laser Bahia and Vago generate far greater side force than those boats with standard symmetric spinnakers. To counter this, these boats need to be sailed downwind with their centreboard/daggerboard fully down. Only in light winds should the board be lifted one third up.

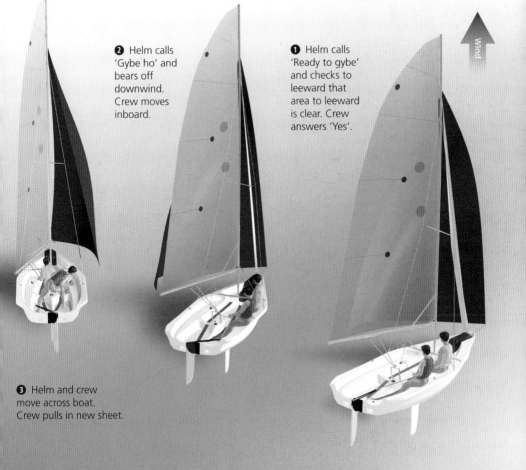

❷ Helm calls 'Gybe ho' and bears off downwind. Crew moves inboard.

❶ Helm calls 'Ready to gybe' and checks to leeward that area to leeward is clear. Crew answers 'Yes'.

Wind

❸ Helm and crew move across boat. Crew pulls in new sheet.

Catamarans

Catamarans like the Dart 16X offer yet another dimension to dinghy sailing. Fast and stable, their performance factor alone is one of their key attractions. They do, however, require different sailing techniques to those used in dinghies, particularly when tacking and sailing fast off wind. One of the most noticeable differences between a catamaran and a dinghy is the apparent wind angle, which swings forward as the catamaran accelerates to the point when even gybing downwind the sails have to be sheeted in as if on a close reach.

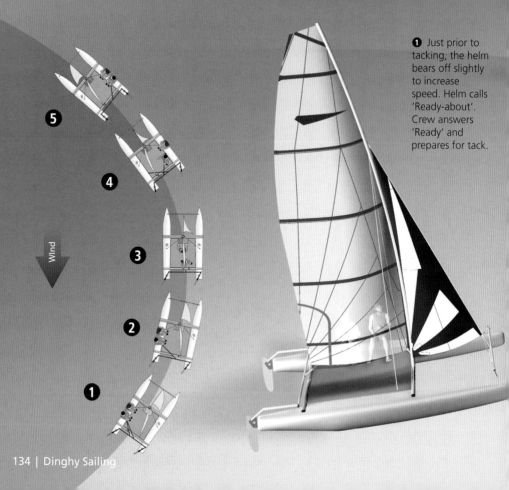

❶ Just prior to tacking, the helm bears off slightly to increase speed. Helm calls 'Ready-about'. Crew answers 'Ready' and prepares for tack.

Wind

⑤ Helm and crew resume their normal positions and trim the sails to suit the new course.

④ Helm eases the mainsheet and changes hands on sheet and tiller extension. If the cat gets trapped in irons, helm must push the tiller on the opposite lock to steer the boat backwards through the eye of the wind. Crew releases the jib sheet as the bows bear round and pulls in on the opposite sheet.

Wind

② Crew uncleats the jib sheet but maintains tension on sheet.

Tacking

Catamarans are notoriously difficult to tack in comparison to dinghies because they do not carry their way when head to wind and can easily end up 'in irons', head to wind.

Sailing upwind

Catamarans sail at their fastest upwind when the windward hull is just 'kissing' the tops of the waves. All the loads are then being carried in the leeward hull and foils, and the windward hull offers minimal resistance.

To keep the cat at this attitude takes practice. When the winds are strong enough for the helm and crew to be trapezing, this heel is maintained by hauling the mainsheet in tight and trimming the sail with the traveller.

Wind

Gybing

Because of their inherent stability and faster speed, gybing a catamaran can be easier than in a performance dinghy in a strong breeze. This is how it is done:

3 Helm and crew resume their normal positions and trim the sails to suit the new course.

2 Helm and crew cross sides, with the helm swinging the extension behind the mainsheet to the opposite side. He then changes hands on tiller extension, and grasps the mainsheet tackle with the other. As the mainsail swings across, the helm arrests the main momentarily to flick the battens to take up their correct curve.

3

2

1

1 Helm calls 'Stand by to gybe' and bears off from broad reach to a downwind run. Crew double-checks that the course ahead is clear and replies 'Yes'. Helm calls 'Gybe-ho' and pushes the tiller over to turn the cat through the wind.

Recovering from a capsize

Catamarans are notoriously difficult to right after a capsize. The key is to move quickly to prevent inversion and possible damage to the rig. This is the routine:

■ One person stands on the leeward centreboard, and holding onto the jib sheet, leans their weight outboard.

■ With catamarans like the Dart 16X, which do not have centreboards, both crew need to stand on the leeward hull.

■ If this fails to right the cat, the second crew can help by standing on the bow or stern of the leeward hull to sink it, which helps to rotate the rig out of the water and right the boat.

■ Once upright, crew release sheets and climb back onboard, resume their positions and course, and set the sails to suit.

Note the fixed righting line attached under the main beam, and second line held by the helm which is attached to the base of the mast and stored in the halyard bag for just these occasions.

Reaching in strong winds

Catamarans are notorious for burying their lee bow which then leads to a capsize or, more spectacular still, a forward pitchpole. Experience in a dinghy teaches you to bear away when the boat becomes over-pressed on a reach, but a catamaran simply accelerates, loading the leeward hull further until the bow buries itself into a wave and trips over. The key is to ease the mainsheet, dropping it altogether if necessary, and then bear away very gently. In strong conditions any change of course other than tacking, should be gentle, because the smallest change of course has such a dramatic effect on the build-up of apparent wind and acceleration of the boat.

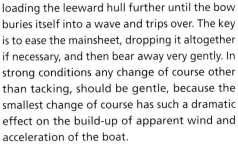

Tuning

What makes a fast boat? Mast settings, sail shape, crew and hull weight, right down to the finish on the hull and foils can all have a direct bearing on boat speed. The best way to start, is to replicate the settings from the fastest boat in your fleet or download a tuning guide from the class website. Most top sailors are only too happy to give novices a helping hand in setting up their boats because the closer the competition at home, the faster they will be at open meetings and championships.

Hull and foils

Dents, scratches and uneven paintwork all have a detrimental effect on the flow of water across the surfaces and cause drag. Check the hull over after every outing, and repair any damage, smoothing out the blemishes with 600 grade wet and dry sandpaper. Many top sailors flatten down the finish on the entire undersides and foils of their boats with 600 paper to minimize induced drag. Never apply polish, for far from inducing better flow across the surface, wax inhibits the barrier flow.

A worn or chipped centreboard like this will have a detrimental effect on performance because the foil is working under high pressure. It should be repaired by filling in with gel paint.

The centreboard and rudder require particular attention because they are working under pressure, which magnifies the problems of imperfections, misalignment or sideways movement. Turn the dinghy on its side and extend the centreboard/daggerboard fully down to check if there is any sloppiness in the case. The board should not have any sideways movement. If it does, then it will need packing out on either side with a hard plastic veneer like Formica or a similar kitchen surface material. Also check how far the board swings down.

The next check is to lay the hull upside down on level ground with centreboard and rudder fully extended to check their vertical alignment. If either is out, then the boat is likely to point higher on one tack than the other.

The bottom of the centreboard slot is another area that can cause significant

Check the vertical alignment of rudder and centreboard/daggerboard. If there is any variation, the boat will point higher on one tack than the other.

turbulence unless fitted with a neoprene rubber or Melamine plastic sealing strip or gasket. These need to fit flush with the bottom of the hull and be kept in good condition because any damage will cause considerable drag.

Hull weight is another important factor. If your boat is beyond a few kilos of the minimum weight set by the class rules, then look at any ways within the rules to lighten ship. There is no advantage in carrying needless weight around.

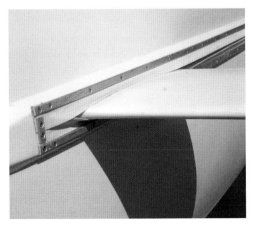

Is the centreboard sealing strip in good condition? Any tears or distortions can cause considerable drag.

The rig

With one-design classes like the Laser family, masts, booms, rigging and sails are all uniform, but in other classes the choice of mast and sails can be open. Masts are available in a variety of sectional shapes and each has different bend characteristics. Generally, the lighter the crew, the bendier the mast needs to be in order to flatten the mainsail, and in some cases where masts have flexible top sections, to spill wind when the rig becomes overpowered. If you have a choice, then ask advice from the fastest team in the fleet with a similar crew weight to your own, and start by following their example.

The first check is to ensure that the mast is a tight fit in its step, and in the case of keel-stepped masts, at the deck gate too. If there is any play at either point, the mast will pivot and bend uncontrollably when sailing, negating all the careful tuning you have undertaken.

Another essential is a log book to note down any setting changes and the benefits these bring when comparing your speed with others.

Sailmakers design their mainsails to match the bend characteristics of each mast, so when ordering a sail, be sure to specify the make and section, as well as your crew weight. The luff is cut with a predetermined amount of pre-bend, so ask the sailmaker for this and any other tuning notes, such as mast rake, spreader settings and shroud tension, and use these as a starting point to tuning the rig.

When replicating rig settings from another boat, start with the mast step measured from the transom. Then turn the boat on its side when fully rigged, and measure the mast rake from tip to transom.

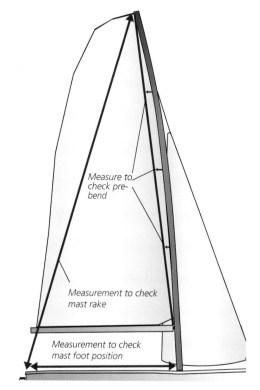

Measure to check pre-bend

Measurement to check mast rake

Measurement to check mast foot position

Pre-bend is gauged by tensioning a line strung between the mast tip and gooseneck, and with the mainsheet and vang released, measuring the maximum bend up the luff. If you are unable to ascertain the optimum amount of pre-bend from your sailmaker, class association or a leading competitor, start with 3-4in (75-100mm). Looking from the head of the sail, you want a uniform section across the full height of the sail. If it is too full or flat in the middle, adjust the pre-bend accordingly, adding more bend to take out the extra fullness, or reducing it if the mid-section of the sail is too flat.

Check that the mainsail has a uniform cross-section throughout its height.

Pre-bend is controlled by the tension in the shrouds, coupled with the angle of the spreaders, which push the shrouds out and aft of the direct line between hounds and chain plate. The angle of sweep back is adjusted at the spreader root. The more the spreaders are swept back, the more the pre-bend.

Spreader length determines sideways stiffness. The more the spreaders push the shrouds out, the stiffer the mast will be. Lighter crews will want less stiffness than heavy crews to allow the top section to bend over to leeward and depower the rig in stronger winds.

Keel-stepped masts can be further controlled at deck level by using chocks or a worm drive to adjust mast bend at the gate while sailing. This is particularly useful in stronger winds, allowing crews to increase bend and flatten the mainsail when sailing upwind, then increase fullness again off wind.

Pre-bend settings on deck-stepped masts are limited to spreader adjustments, unless the boat is equipped with an extra set of lower shrouds between shroud and gooseneck as on the Bahia.

Lower shrouds

This procedure should be completed without the mainsail hoisted or the boom attached to the mast. With the boat on the shore, jib up and rig tension on, the lower shroud wires should be just tight enough to hold the mast straight in both fore/aft and side to side planes.

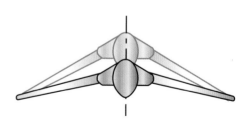

Spreader angle controls pre-bend. The greater the angle, the more the bend.

Forestay tension. Calibration marks on the mast allow you to replicate tension, or make small adjustments.

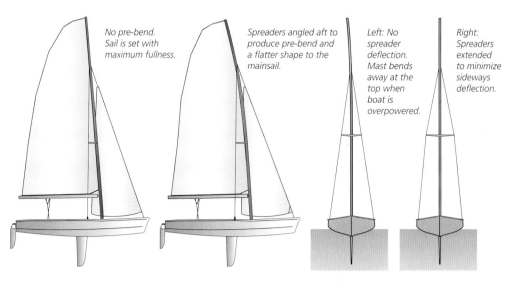

No pre-bend. Sail is set with maximum fullness.

Spreaders angled aft to produce pre-bend and a flatter shape to the mainsail.

Left: No spreader deflection. Mast bends away at the top when boat is overpowered.

Right: Spreaders extended to minimize sideways deflection.

Spreader angle. A series of pre-drilled holes allows you to make small adjustments.

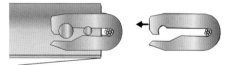

Spreader ends can be adjusted for length.

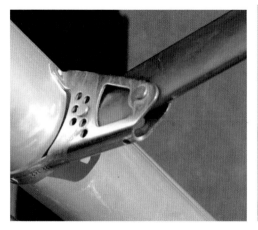

Rig tension

This is applied using the jib halyard purchase system. A tension gauge offers the most accurate way to measure this and replicate the settings, but if you don't possess one of these, the following procedure works well for most conditions.

1. Lean into the boat and sight up the sail luff groove on the mast. Lower shroud settings should be checked and readjusted whenever a new optimum rig tension setting is established.

2. Sail the boat upwind in a medium breeze just sufficient to support both helm and crew in their appropriate hiking or trapezing positions.

3. Observe the visual tension exhibited by the leeward shroud wire.

4. Stop the boat and either increase or decrease the rig tension using the jib halyard purchase system until the leeward shroud is just visibly tight when repeating steps 2 and 3.

5. Mark the vertical position of the jib halyard tension system hook in relation to the aft face of the mast in order to repeat the setting, and note it in your log book.

Tip

Keep a note of all changes to rig tension and sheet settings in a pocket book, and never change more than one setting at a time, otherwise you will never be sure what adjustment made the boat go faster or slower.

This procedure will provide a competitive, well-supported, dynamic rig on any asymmetric dinghy without the use of a rig tension gauge. Try it; you'll be surprised how fast and effective this single setting is across the wind range.

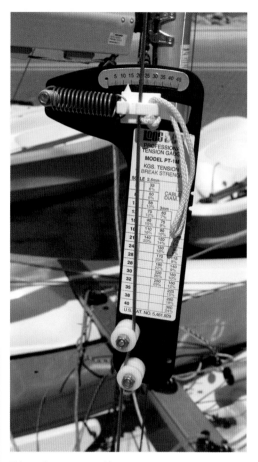

This tension gauge provides an accurate measure of rig tension.

Jib

With the jib sheeted in to a nominal close-hauled position, mark the sheet with a permanent marker just ahead of where it passes through the jib sheet fairlead. Then correspond this mark accurately to the opposing jib sheet. This marker will now serve as a visual tuning aid and reference point from one tack to the other on any given day, especially when used in association with a calibration sticker or marks. It also provides a valuable tutorial/reference point when sailing with less experienced crews.

Telltales

Telltales set in the jib close to the luff provide a very good visual indicator to the helm when beating to windward and the jib is sheeted in hard. Ideally, the two light strips of wool or nylon cloth set on either side of the sail, should fly parallel as in ❷ .

When sailing off the wind, the telltales give a visual to the crew on whether to tighten sheets ❶ or ease them out ❸.

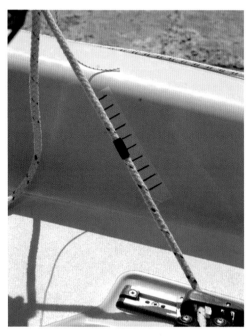

Calibration marks provide a simple visual for the crew when setting sheet tension.

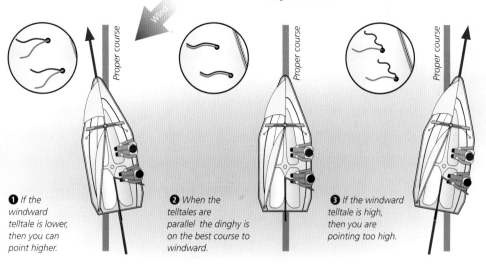

❶ *If the windward telltale is lower, then you can point higher.*

❷ *When the telltales are parallel the dinghy is on the best course to windward.*

❸ *If the windward telltale is high, then you are pointing too high.*

Mainsail

Hoist the mainsail until its head is positioned hard against the mast head cap to ensure maximum sail projection and best fit on the rig. Ensure any stretch in the halyard is removed prior to operating any other sail controls.

Nominally set the outhaul a hand's width inside the black band or maximum foot length along the boom. As the wind increases, depower the boat by increasing the outhaul tension incrementally until the foot is tight.

Set the Cunningham downhaul to remove 75% of the horizontal creases in the luff area of the sail. As the wind increases depower the boat by increasing tension until all the horizontal creases are removed and the luff area of the sail looks visually tighter than the central, main body of the sail.

Tension the kicker/vang system so that the mid/upper leech telltales stream solidly for 80% of the time and stall slightly for 20% of the time when sailing upwind. As the wind increases, kicker/vang tension will also have to be increased to maintain this status. When the boat feels overpowered, ease the kicker/vang until the leech telltales stream freely 100% of the time. Easing even more kicker/vang tension will depower the boat

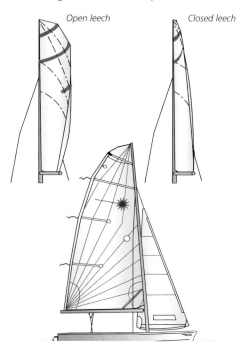

Open leech   Closed leech

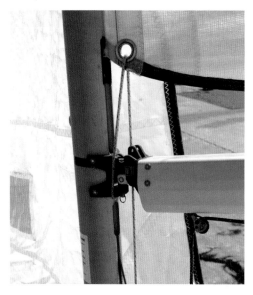

Cunningham tension: This controls the aerofoil shape of the sail. Increased tension flattens the sail, providing a better shape for sailing upwind. Release it when sailing offwind.

Vang tension controls the shape of the leech. The telltales set on the end of the battens provide a visual check.

further, though this will also increase the pressure on the mainsheet, making it hard to manage the sail!

Gennaker

A stopper knot/bobble should always be used in the gennaker tack line to ensure that the sail cannot get closer than 3–4in (75–100mm) to the end of the bowsprit. This ensures that the tack of the sail cannot become held fast on the wrong side of the gennaker pole after gybing. It also helps to power the sail up by decreasing tension in the luff and producing

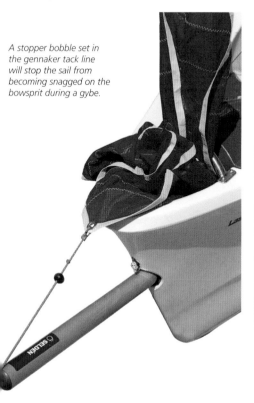

A stopper bobble set in the gennaker tack line will stop the sail from becoming snagged on the bowsprit during a gybe.

a proportionally tighter leech. As an added bonus it gives greater sail to water clearance when crashing down larger waves in strong winds.

Rudder

The rudder should always be in a 100% down position to optimize control, feel and performance. Just after launching, always lean over the back of the boat and push the rudder blade down by hand prior to tightening up and cleating the rudder downhaul line. This is the only way you can be certain the rudder blade is fully extended.

Centreboard/Daggerboard

This should always be used in the fully down position when sailing to windward to optimize control, feel and performance.

Tip

Asymmetric dinghies are capable of creating significant foil lift when driven hard. On asymmetric dinghies with centreboards it is often advisable to fit an elastic centreboard retaining leash with snap hook. When positioning the centreboard after launching, simply attach the snap hook onto the centreboard rope handle to prevent the foil from riding up when travelling at high speed.

Heavy weather sailing

This is when sailing is at its most exhilarating, but the techniques to maximize speed and minimize the chance of capsizing come only with practice.

The boat will be under considerable stress, so check all the gear before setting out so that nothing is likely to break, and wear waterproof clothing. Sailing in strong winds can sap your strength and stamina, so if you start to become tired or cold, head for shore. Most important of all, ensure that there is a safety boat monitoring the fleet that will come to your aid in the event of a capsize.

Reaching

- If possible, start out on a reach, the easiest point of sailing in heavy weather, to get used to the conditions.

- Leave the centreboard up and bring crew weight well aft to lift the bow and encourage the boat to plane.

- The mainsail and jib will require constant adjustment, easing them out and bearing away when overpowered, then luffing back up during the lulls.

- Play the waves like a windsurfer, pumping the mainsail once when bearing away on the crest, to get on the plane, then pointing up and sheeting in again to maintain this attitude on the wave for as long as possible.

Well balanced with crew playing the gennaker sheet and helm easing the mainsheet to match the course and changes in wind strength.

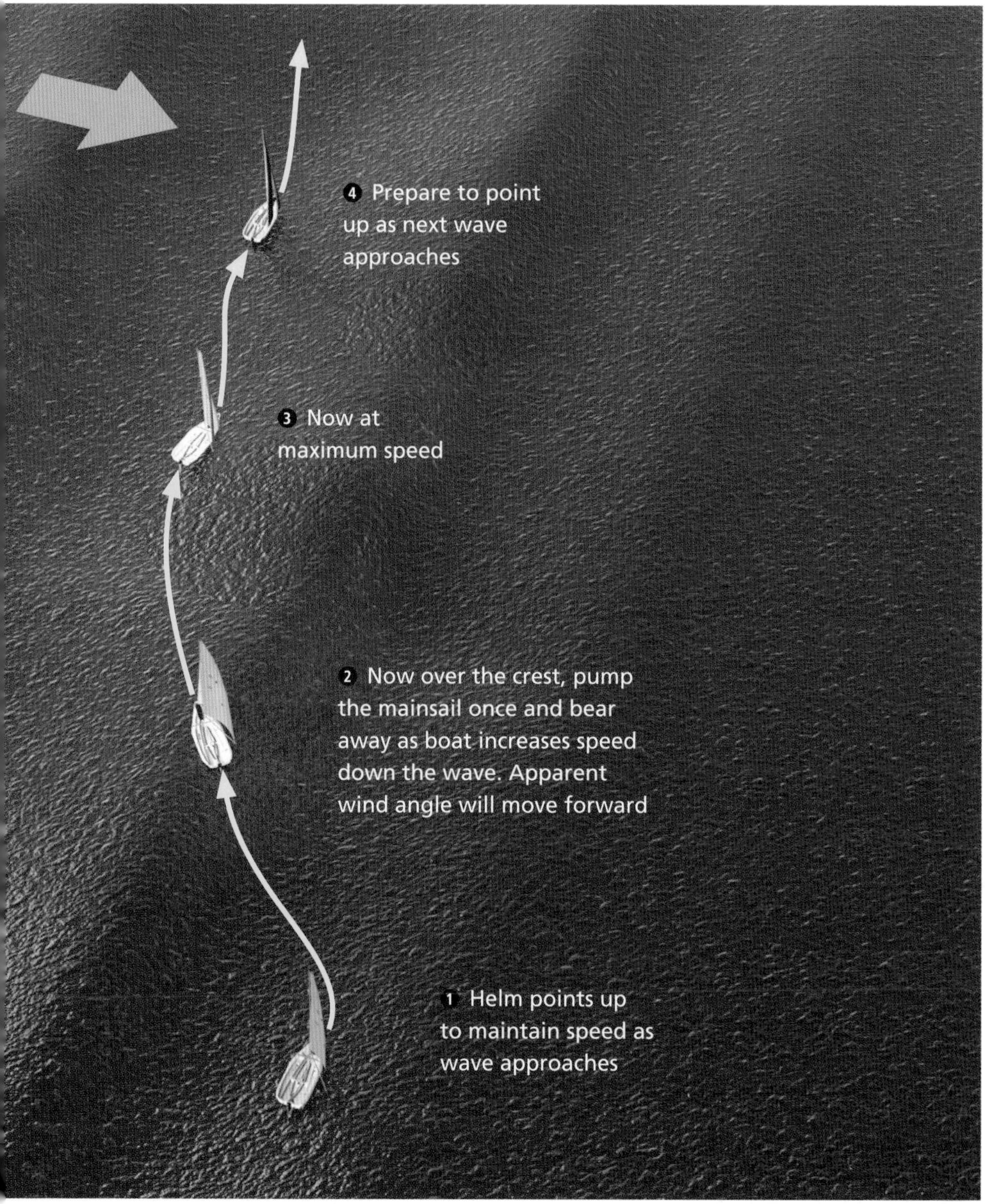

4 Prepare to point
up as next wave
approaches

3 Now at
maximum speed

2 Now over the crest, pump
the mainsail once and bear
away as boat increases speed
down the wave. Apparent
wind angle will move forward

1 Helm points up
to maintain speed as
wave approaches

Move your body weight forward as the dinghy climbs on the crest of the wave, then pump the mainsail to accelerate the boat down the back of the wave, moving your weight aft again to encourage surfing.

Running downwind

- Bring crew weight well aft to lift the bow and encourage the boat to plane. The mainsail and spinnaker will require constant adjustment, easing them out and bearing away when overpowered, then luffing back up during the lulls. Leaving centreboard/daggerboard down will give greater stability and control.
- Play the waves, first bearing away on the crest, then pointing up to maintain this attitude on the wave for as long as possible.
- The yacht racing rules allow you to pump the sails once on each wave to encourage planing.
- When sailing downwind, the boom kicker/vang should be eased to open the roach of the mainsail and encourage a clean airflow across the full length of the leech. Beware of letting the boom too far out, because if the head of the sail is allowed to set forward of the mast, this can lead to a windward roll and capsize.
- If the dinghy begins to roll wildly, sheeting in the mainsail will dampen the movement.

Going...going...

...gone. When the dinghy starts doing a death roll, it is because the mainsail is let out too far. Pulling the sheet in a small amount will stop the roll.

Gybing

- This requires close coordination and communication between the crew.
- Time the manoeuvre when the boat is sailing at its fastest over a flat area between waves. Never attempt to gybe when the boat has slowed or is in the trough of a wave because wind pressure on the rig will be at its greatest and more than likely lead to a capsize.
- As the boom starts to swing across, move smartly to the new windward side to balance out the heeling force of the mainsail as it slams across.

❶ Head up as the boat climbs the wave to maintain speed

❷ Pump the mainsail to accelerate away down the wave

Judge your gybe at the mark when conditions are right, and do not allow others to pressure you into a premature move. It will almost certainly lead to a capsize.

If you can sail an Optimist in these conditions, you can sail any boat!

4 Prepare to climb the next wave

3 Time the gybe to coincide with when the boat is sailing fast and in flat water

Time your gybe when the boat is going at its fastest.

Perfect timing...riding a downward wave around the gybe mark.

Head up as wave approaches to present the minimum surface area.

As the wave passes start to bear off again...

...and continue on normal close-hauled angle to the wind.

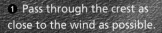

1 Pass through the crest as close to the wind as possible.

2 Bear off for maximum speed

Close-hauled

- When sailing at closer angles to the wind, bring crew weight forward to the point of maximum beam and sheet the jib in hard. With the crew fully extended and centreboard down, the helm than trims the mainsail to balance the boat, spilling wind when overpressed. To prevent further heeling, point the boat higher into the wind until the jib luff lifts to ease the pressure on the rig and gain ground to windward.
- When steering though big waves, luff up as the boat climbs the crest and bear away down the back of the wave.

3 Prepare to luff up as the wave approaches,

Tacking

Look for an area of flat water between waves and start the manoeuvre as soon as the boat has passed through the crest so that you have time to complete the tack before the next wave hits.

❶ Prepare to luff up as the wave approaches.

Tacking in heavy weather requires close coordination. Give the crew plenty of warning and turn into the tack gradually.

Keep a close eye on other boats around you and give yourself plenty of room to tack.

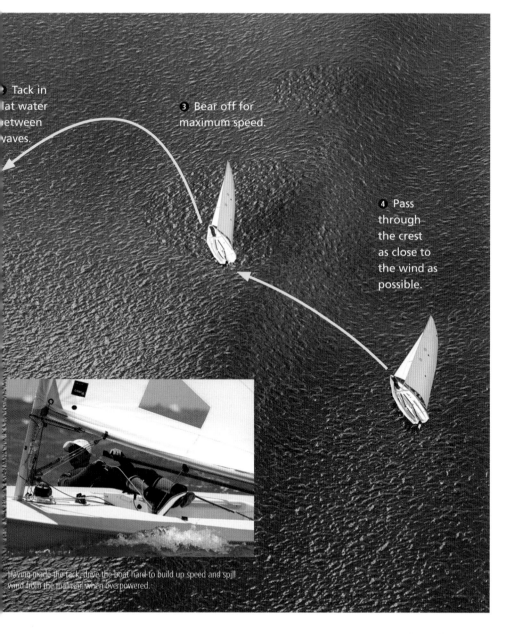

Tack in flat water between waves.

3 Bear off for maximum speed.

4 Pass through the crest as close to the wind as possible.

Having made the tack, drive the boat hard to build up speed and spill wind from the mainsail when overpowered.

Basics
of racing

Racing, they say, improves the breed. It is certainly one of the best ways to improve your sailing skills and adds a new dimension to the sport. If you have joined a club, then you will be welcomed into their racing fleet, even if the learning curve is steep to start with.

The start

The basics of racing

You will need to bone up on the yacht racing rules, which are a subject of their own. Consult *The Yacht Racing Rules 2009-12* by Bryan Willis and his abridged *Companion*, which is printed on waterproof paper to take afloat with you.

Preparation and practice are the keys to performance, but it is pre-race planning that most often determines winner from also-ran. There is rarely little to divide the top few boats as far as performance is concerned, but the silverware invariably goes to the crew that has done most to bone up on weather patterns and local conditions, as well as put in the practice time that makes teamwork needle sharp.

Luck plays its part too, but over a series of races this has a habit of balancing out. Those who do their homework before racing – charting tidal streams, spotting wind bends and other local nuances – are likely to minimize the bad breaks and always turn good luck to its fullest advantage.

Start by developing a checklist for the boat. When racing at sea, most clubs insist on you carrying an anchor, towline and paddle, and life jackets or buoyancy aids are now compulsory wherever you sail.

Checklist
☑ Lifejackets/buoyancy aids
☑ Sails
☑ Battens
☑ Rudder and tiller
☑ Sheets
☑ Protest flag
☑ Timing watch
☑ Bailer and sponge
☑ Food and water
☑ Spare shackles and line

Before you set out, take a note of the course, timings for the start and any changes in tidal stream, which are invariably linked to local high and low water times. You can write this down on a waterproof tablet with a chinagraph or similar water-soluble pencil to take in the boat with you, or simply scribble it down on an area of the deck where it won't get rubbed off during the race. Some clubs insist that you sign in for a race as well as sign out once back on shore, so check that too before setting sail.

Leave enough time to at least sail up the first leg to identify the windward mark

and check out any wind bends or fluctuations and any impact that the tidal stream is likely to have.

Unless the course area is set several miles offshore, the land can influence the wind. Check its direction when leaving the beach or bank, and again at the course extremities for any variations. A preliminary sail around the course will reveal bends in the airflow, particularly where there are folds in the landscape. In many coastal areas, the wind direction is known to swing progressively through the day, essential knowledge when it comes to deciding which side of the course is likely to pay during the beat, reach and running legs. A permanent change often signifies a wind bend rather than a swing in direction. The clues come from watching other dinghies in the area. If they are heading at differing angles, a bend in the airflow is likely, especially if the course

is set close inshore. This information could well dictate the favoured tack towards the mark. Check also the wind gusts to see if they are heading or freeing. On squally days the cat's paws on the water that herald their arrival will be the clue for going about to gain most from the freeing tack.

One note of caution though; if winds are light, stay in the vicinity of the starting area during the last 15 minutes before the gun, keeping an eye on the committee boat for any change to the course. This is also the time to take in high protein food and drink so that it is absorbed within the body before the start, to provide that extra pep and energy when it is required most. While eating these rations, use the time to discuss strategy, check out the start line and its angle to the wind, and ready the watch to synchronize with the initial warning signal.

First warning signal before the start

Bang..! The countdown has begun either 10 or 5 minutes before the start. Luff up head to wind somewhere along the line where you can see the committee boat and pin end to check if one end of the start line is more favoured than the other. Other factors to take into account are:

? Is the current more favourable at one end than the other?

? Are the gusts stronger at one side of the course?

? Can the first mark be laid in one tack?

? Does the start timing coincide with expected oscillations in wind direction?

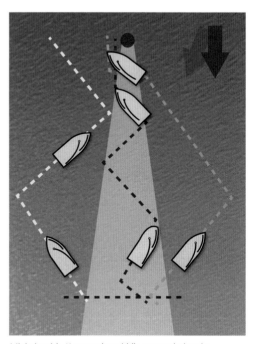

Minimize risk. Keep to the middle course during the first beat, playing the shifts as they come, and monitor the performance of those on either flank to gauge any advantage.

Planning first leg strategy

A race series is won by minimizing risk, not by taking miracle-seeking flyers to one side of the course, particularly on the first beat. Unless tide or wind clearly favour one side, it invariably pays to take a middle path up the first beat, while monitoring the performance of those on either flank to gauge any advantages. If the weather forecast or your own observations indicate that a wind shift is likely, beat up to the mark in a sector 10° towards the favoured side, tacking on the oscillating shifts as they occur. If, after completing half the distance, it becomes apparent that conditions on the other side of the course present a significant advantage it will not be too late to cross over. The lead will doubtless be held by another boat, but having

made a good start and played the percentages you will still be in a challenging position, which is more than can be said for those that gambled on the opposite side of the course!

The start

Accurate timing, clear air and boat speed are the key ingredients for that perfect start, but achieving this in the highly charged atmosphere of a big fleet takes practice and a degree of aggressiveness that many helmsmen lack. A moment's hesitation or sign of timidness as other dinghies converge on the line, all fighting for pole position during the closing seconds before the gun, is a sure passport to the second row, leaving you with the unenviable task of fighting a path through the choppy wake and wind shadow cast by those ahead.

During this final countdown, the prime job of the crew is to call out the time at 15-second intervals during the final five minutes, and at five-second intervals during the last minute, and warn the helm of oncoming dinghies hidden from view, especially after the five-minute gun when the racing rules come into play.

The crew is also best placed to judge the dinghy's relative position to the line and ensure that the boat does not cross early, especially

if a One Minute Rule is in operation, earning instant disqualification for line jumpers.

Timed run

One of the most tried and tested methods of hitting the line on cue is the timed run start. Having pinpointed the favoured end of the line, the strategy is to sail off on a reciprocal course to the final close-hauled approach for a set time. A one-minute run is often best because it does not take you too far from the line. Allow a further 10 seconds to tack and regain speed and two minutes ten seconds later you will have your bows on the line.

By practising a series of timed runs in the 15 minutes before the start, the helm can get an accurate idea of the time required to allow for tacking in that day's conditions.

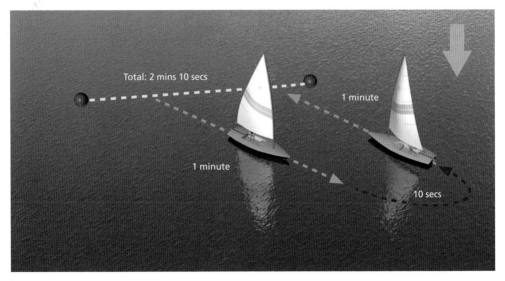

The timed run: Reach away from the line for one minutes. Allow 10 seconds to tack, then return close-hauled to cross the line 2 minutes 10 seconds after starting your run.

Avoid the crush.
Start in clear air

If the line is biased to one side or the other, ease sheets to avoid the build-up and start a little lower down the line.

Avoid the wind
shadow of other
boats

Reaching starts

In level boat or one-design racing, the golden rule is to start at the leeward end of a reaching start line, for boats at the pin end will be sailing a closer and thus faster course to the wind than their opposite numbers to windward. Also, by having the apparent wind further forward, the boat to leeward is less likely to be affected by the wind shadow cast by other boats around them. The exception to this rule comes when sailing a small boat in a mixed fleet for, however good a start, the larger dinghies quickly break through, blanketing the wind. The only way to avoid this is to start on the weather side of the fleet, sailing high to maintain clear air before setting a course directly for the next mark once the threat from larger boats has receded.

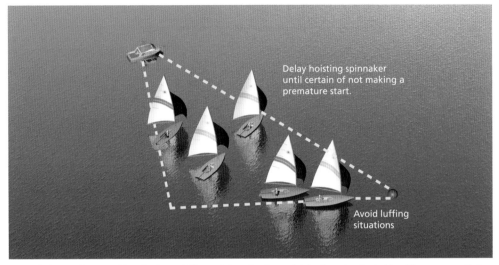

Delay hoisting spinnaker until certain of not making a premature start.

Avoid luffing situations

Downwind starts: Try to avoid getting into a luffing match on the line and delay the spinnaker hoist until you are sure that you will not cross the line early.

Downwind starts

The timed run – sailing close-hauled away from the line and returning on a broad reach – also works well for downwind starts. Not hoisting the spinnaker until the last moment will give you the freedom to luff others that threaten your wind or to exploit an opening in the line of boats, but make sure you are ready to make a fast set, otherwise that clear air advantage will be lost.

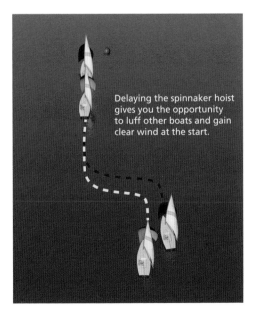

Delaying the spinnaker hoist gives you the opportunity to luff other boats and gain clear wind at the start.

Around the course

First beat strategy

The first few minutes after any start should be spent extracting maximum speed from the dinghy. Never put in a tack unless you are completely blocked ahead, for more ground will be lost manoeuvring in the confused wind and wave conditions immediately after the start than by bearing off a few points, easing sheets, and driving clear of the wind shadow cast by competing boats. Unless conditions change dramatically, never be drawn from your original strategy. If port is the freeing tack and you find yourself on a collision course with another boat on starboard, give way. It is better to lose two boat lengths bearing away under its stern than tack to leeward and lose the initiative to choose your own course.

Both helm and crew need to monitor the compass and be prepared to tack whenever the wind heads more than 5°. The

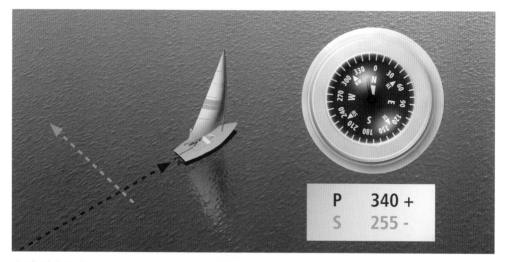

P   340 +
S   255 -

Play the shifts: Write the mean compass headings for each tack close to the compass with a plus next to the port figure and a minus against the starboard number. When the heading reads above the starboard figure (and below on port tack) you are enjoying a freeing shift.

wind plays all manner of tricks and you must learn to differentiate between shifts that head momentarily before returning to their previous direction and more stable changes. The simplest way to avoid being tricked into tacking is to hold a 30-second moratorium after the shift occurs. This not only gives time for the wind to settle, but warns the crew to be ready for a fast tack when the decision is made. It is a good idea to write the mean compass headings for each tack on self-adhesive plastic sheets stuck on either side of the deck, close to the compass, with a plus sign against the port figure and a minus sign against the starboard heading. This gives a visual reminder that when the compass heading reads above the mean starboard figure (and below on port tack) the boat is enjoying a freeing wind.

A gusting wind generally veers in the northern hemisphere to lift boats on starboard, but backs in the southern hemisphere to favour those on port tack. Crews with the foresight to cross over to the favoured tack as the cat's paws approach are likely to enjoy an immediate advantage over those who wait for the compass to tell them of the change. In these circumstances that 30-second tacking rule can be dispensed with, but only if this generalization was borne out during the pre-race check on conditions, for there can be exceptions, especially if the course is set close inshore where wind patterns become confused by the land.

Tidal stream

A current of water across the course adds another dimension to first leg strategy, and

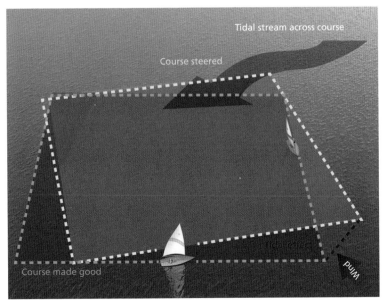

Tidal stream across the course adds another dimension to upwind strategy. Exploit any variations in the strength of stream by staying inshore if the adverse current is stronger further out to sea for instance, and keep a visual bearing on a landmark or buoy to keep a check on the tidal effect.

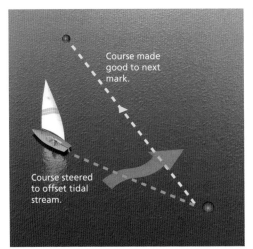

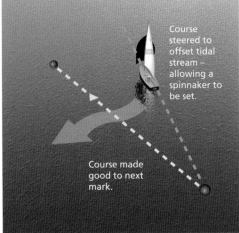

Course steered to offset tidal stream.

Course steered to offset tidal stream. Course over the ground allows crew to ease sheets or even carry a spinnaker.

variations in strength and direction must be recognized before the start. Remember, the strength and direction of the current are certain, the wind is not, so the first boat to tack towards the favoured side will take a progressive advantage over the fleet. Only a major shift or increase in wind speed will be great enough to counteract even a ½ knot variation in tidal stream. There are many areas of the world where the current can flow at between 2 and 4 knots, so this is an essential element to be taken into consideration when race strategy is planned.

The lee bow myth

It is a common misconception that when the bows are angled to weather of the tidal stream, the boat is pushed dramatically to windward by the lift effect of the water passing

Always eyeball the next mark. Don't simply follow the leader - they may not have allowed for tidal affect.

over the aerofoil section of the centreboard/ daggerboard. Unfortunately, this lee bow effect is pure myth. The confusion arises from the fact that when a dinghy is faced with an offset tidal stream, the duration of the two tacks alters, for the boat beating into an adverse current will take longer to cover the same distance than an opposing dinghy takes on the opposite tack. But the current is nothing more than a moving escalator and boats tacking to one side of the course or the other will remain relative to each other. The only gains to be made are from exploiting variations in the strength of this current, because of the effect this has on the wind over the ground.

Comeback strategy

After a bad start or collision, picking up places is as much a state of mind as anything else. Remain dejected or angry and you fail to spot the opportunities to regain that lost ground. Treat the situation calmly by turning attention to the breaks rather than misfortune, and a comeback is assured. After a poor start, the first task must be to break into clear air. A tack onto port, ducking under opposing boats to break into clear air will lose less ground than remaining boxed in for much of the first leg, and if the tack back onto starboard can be timed to coincide with the positioning of another starboard tacker ahead and to leeward, it will block other

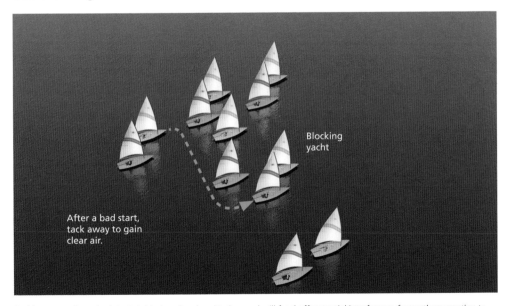

Blocking
yacht

After a bad start,
tack away to gain
clear air.

Tacking away after a bad start. A blocker ahead and to leeward will fend off potential interference from others wanting to cross just ahead and tack on your wind. When tacking back, position yourself to weather of competitors nearby so that you are free to play the shifts.

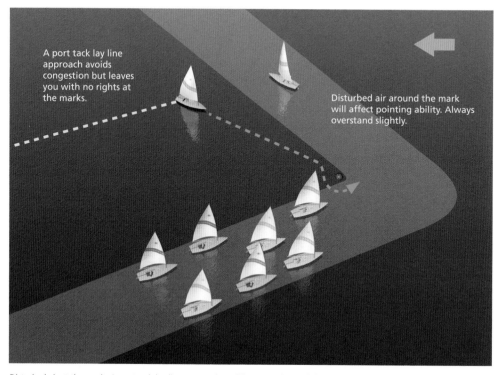

A port tack lay line approach avoids congestion but leaves you with no rights at the marks.

Disturbed air around the mark will affect pointing ability. Always overstand slightly.

Disturbed air at the mark. A port tack lay line approach avoids congestion and the dirty wind of those boats ahead, but leaves you with no rights at the mark.

boats from tacking under your lee bow and disturbing the air.

Clear air is a high priority but so too are the shifts, and while it may be difficult to discern any pattern in the confused conditions midway down the fleet, the sooner you can time the tacks to coincide with the oscillations in the wind, the faster the recovery.

When approaching the windward mark the greatest gains can often be made by avoiding the majority of the fleet, all sailing in each other's dirty wind, stacked up on the starboard lay line. One optioon is to approach the lay line on port tack just short of the mark and find a hole to tack in if necessary. Remember that in the disturbed air around the mark, pointing ability will be impaired, so always overstand slightly to avoid being squeezed out at the turn.

The downwind leg
Before rounding the weather mark, brief the crew on whether the spinnaker is required, and on what gybe.

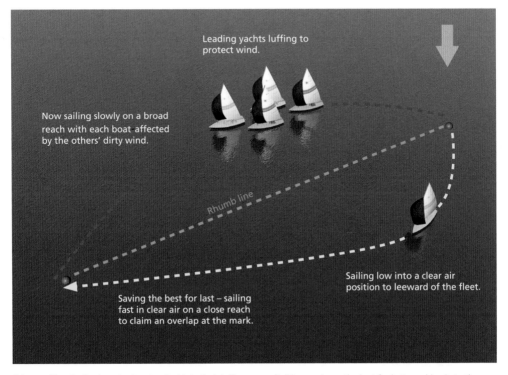

Leading yachts luffing to protect wind.

Now sailing slowly on a broad reach with each boat affected by the others' dirty wind.

Rhumb line

Sailing low into a clear air position to leeward of the fleet.

Saving the best for last – sailing fast in clear air on a close reach to claim an overlap at the mark.

When trailing the leaders, don't get sucked into their luffing game. Sail low and save the best for last, reaching in to the gybe mark while those to windward are forced to steer a broader, slower line to the mark.

The task for the leading crew will be to sail the fastest course, maintaining a blocking position between the fleet and the next mark, but for those astern other options abound.

Saving the best for last is a principle that should remain foremost in the mind on any reaching leg. By deviating to leeward soon after rounding the windward mark, you not only avoid the inevitable drift to weather of the rhumb line as each of the leading boats luffs into clear air, but you can keep the faster sailing angle to the last, giving you the speed to maintain, or claim, an overlap three lengths from the gybe mark.

Reaching low after the gybe will rob you of that all important overlap advantage at the leeward mark, so the leading dinghy inevitably maintains a position covering competitors nearest to weather. For those behind, however, a close rounding of the mark to ensure a weather position on those astern and ahead is more important

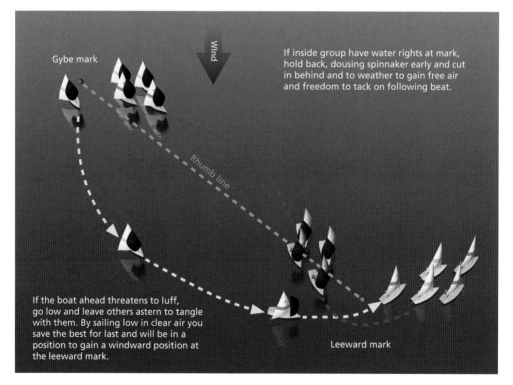

Gybe mark

Wind

If inside group have water rights at mark, hold back, dousing spinnaker early and cut in behind and to weather to gain free air and freedom to tack on following beat.

Rhumb line

If the boat ahead threatens to luff, go low and leave others astern to tangle with them. By sailing low in clear air you save the best for last and will be in a position to gain a windward position at the leeward mark.

Leeward mark

Tactics at the leeward mark

than any final overlap advantage. If there is a tight bunch making a final approach, the chances are that the luffing that will have undoubtedly occurred during the preceding leg will, in extreme cases, have brought the leaders round to the point of almost running down towards the mark, the slowest point of sailing. By saving the best for last, approaching the mark from further to leeward on a broad reach in clear air, there is always the chance of breaking ahead of those further to weather. If an

overlap cannot be claimed not all is lost, for by taking the spinnaker down early if necessary and holding back, it is possible to cut in behind and to weather of the leading bunch, caught up in the confusion of the moment, and quickly break into clear air on the second beat.

The second windward leg
With the first round complete and pecking order established, the leading crew must cover their nearest rivals throughout the second

Covering tactics: A places a blanket cover on B to persuade her to tack. A then rewards B by sailing a little further before tacking to give B clear air. This is repeated when C attempts to cross on port tack.

beat, maintaining a position midway between the weather mark and the fleet, while those astern try to exploit any advantage from a change in conditions or a tactical slip made by those ahead.

Try to ascertain which is the freeing tack prior to rounding the leeward mark, to ensure that no time is lost getting in phase with the oscillating breeze. For the fleet leader the situation becomes complicated when his nearest rivals split tacks, making it impossible to cover every eventuality. First instincts are to continue covering the nearest boat, even if this means tacking into a heading shift, but this only plays into the hands of the third-placed crew. If the boats are close together and of equal speed, the only means available to the leading crew to dictate the course from ahead is to place a blanket cover on the crew making the wrong tactical move to force them to go about. Then, like training mice, reward them for making the right decision with a loose cover to give them little or no disturbed wind. They soon get the message. If these herding tactics are played right, the leading boat will be able to maintain its position midway between the windward mark and its nearest competitors, firmly in control of the situation.

For those further astern, however, the first priority after rounding the leeward mark will be to gain clear wind, get into phase with the oscillating shifts, and wait for those ahead to make mistakes. There is often much to learn from those further to windward, especially in light, fluky conditions when the shifting wind can be difficult to discern. Those leaders make good scouts, pinpointing the lulls and shifting wind.

The run
The downwind leg is no time to sit back and relax once the spinnaker is set. In contrast to the parading reaches, the run provides one of the best opportunities for following crews to pull themselves up through the fleet. It can be a taxing time for the leading crew, who must not only protect their position from the blanketing effects of spinnakers lined up astern, but also stay in phase with the shifting wind. Indeed, playing the shifts is as important downwind as it is on the beat with strategy a mirror image of the tactics employed on the upwind leg. Thus, to start on the run in phase, take up the opposite gybe to the lifted tack immediately after rounding the weather mark.

Monitoring the wind carefully throughout this leg also helps to make the best of the next beat. For instance, if the wind favours the starboard gybe, an immediate gain can be made on less observant competitors by remaining on port tack after rounding the leeward mark – and tacking onto

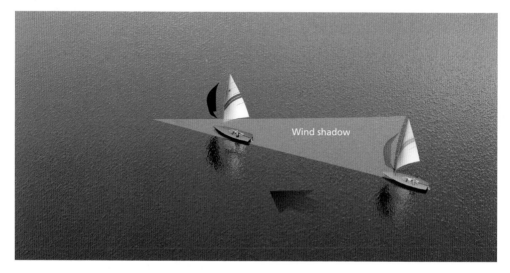
Wind shadow

The wind shadow cast by a dinghy running downwind can affect the wind for a distance of five boat lengths.

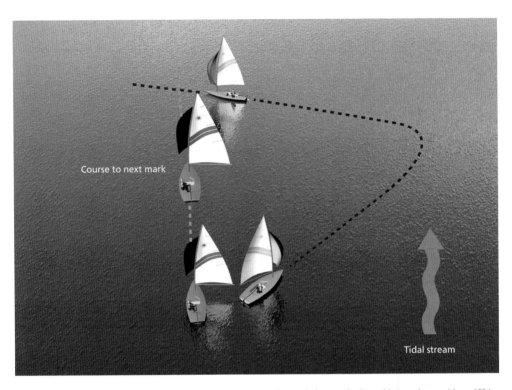

Course to next mark

Tidal stream

A fair tidal stream will cut down the apparent wind when running down wind, necessitating gybing angles as wide as 40° in order to maintain airflow across the sails.

starboard as soon as possible when the port gybe is favoured.

The blanketing effect from a spinnaker casts a wind shadow up to five boat lengths ahead, which the leading crew must evade at all costs, while at the same time duplicating a challenger's every move in order to maintain a covering position between their opponent and the next mark. By contrast, those astern have the advantage of being the first to benefit from each fresh gust and will want to trap the leaders in their shadow, to force them to

gybe out of phase with the shifts and break off the cover. Just like chess, these moves and countermoves call for foresight and sharp thinking which, for many, becomes one of the more enjoyable aspects of dinghy racing.

Tidal stream is another important factor to take into account on this downwind leg. If the current is favourable it reduces the true wind speed, necessitating wide tacks away from the rhumb line to increase apparent wind, especially in light airs when gybing angles as wide as 40° are justified.

When fighting an adverse current the apparent wind effect is increased, allowing a much smaller gybing angle, but the effect of wind against tide can also create a short, choppy sea which, in moderate weather especially, may require a wider tacking angle than normal to ease pitching and keep sails filled.

The final beat

After rounding the leeward mark the sole preoccupation for the leading crew will be to maintain an effective cover over their nearest pursuers, keeping themselves

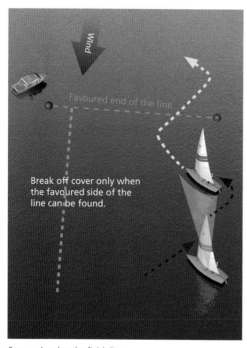

Break off cover only when the favoured side of the line can be found.

Favoured end at the finish line.

between the finish line and the fleet, copying the movement of their closest rivals as soon as a clear weather advantage can be gained. Never be the first to tack on a header. Rather, wait for those behind to make their move, then tack to cover once a weather overlap can be established to negate any chance of the underdog gaining a weather advantage, should the wind continue to shift round.

If boats from another class are approaching the finish ahead, keep a wary eye open for any significant shifts in the wind that might favour one side of the course. This is especially important if the chasing group splits tacks, making it difficult to cover both extremes. Those leading dinghies may also provide a useful pointer to any bias at the finish line. Whatever the case, never overstand the final tack, even if this means breaking cover on those astern, for this only gives away valuable distance, and possibly the lead, to a third boat that may have split tacks to approach the finish unopposed from the opposite side of the course.

For those out of touch with the leading group but still mindful of a respectable finish, the temptation to take a flyer in the hope of a miracle can be strong. But winning a series calls for consistent results and unless there are good reasons to suggest an immediate and dramatic change in conditions, the risks involved are unwarranted. Greater success is likely from playing the shifts accurately while those ahead tack and counter-tack to cover their nearest rivals, often with total disregard for the oscillating wind.

Glossary of terms

A

ABACK – When the jib is sheeted to the windward side and the dinghy is hove-to.

ABAFT – Behind or towards the stern.

ABEAM – At right angles to the boat.

AFT – See Abaft.

AIRFLOW – Flow of air across the sails.

ALTO – Middle-level cloud base.

ALTOCUMULUS – Middle-level cloud.

ALTOSTRATUS – Middle-level cloud.

AMIDSHIPS – Centre of the boat.

ABOUT – To go about is to tack the dinghy through the wind.

ANCHOR – Portable device to moor the dinghy in open water on the end of a line.

ANEMOMETER – Instrument to measure wind speed.

ANTICYCLONE – Meteorological term describing area of high pressure.

APPARENT WIND – The wind experienced by a moving boat. If the boat is stationary, the apparent wind is the same as the true wind. If the boat is moving towards the wind, the apparent wind is greater than the true wind. If the boat is moving away from the wind, the apparent wind is less than the true wind.

ASPECT RATIO – The aspect ratio of a sail is its width measured against its depth of curvature, or height compared to its width. Hence, a high aspect ratio mainsail refers to a tall narrow shape.

ASYMMETRIC SPINNAKER – Downwind sail with a fixed luff, which is tacked or gybed like a jib.

B

BACKING THE JIB – Setting the jib on the weather side to encourage the boat to bear away.

BACKWIND – When the airflow across the jib causes the mainsail to flutter.

BAILER – Scoop to remove water from inside the boat.

BALANCE – Reference to relative balance between the hydrostatic lift on the hull and the central point of the rig. This is measured by the degree of weight or pressure on the tiller, giving weather helm when too heavy and boat wants to point up, and lee helm when too light and boat wants to bear away.

BATTEN – Flexible strip of wood or reinforced resin to stiffen the leech of the sail.

BEAM – Mid part of the dinghy, or measurement of maximum width of the hull.

BEAM REACH – Sailing with the wind directly abeam.

BEAR AWAY – To turn the bows away from the wind.

BEARING – Compass direction.

BEAT – The close-hauled, zigzag course to windward.

BEATING – Sailing close-hauled to windward.

BEAUFORT SCALE – Scale of wind speeds devised by Admiral Sir Francis Beaufort.

BECKET – A second eye or attachment point in a pulley block.

BERMUDA RIG – Single masted sail plan with tall, triangular mainsail.

BIGHT – An open loop in a rope.

BLACK BANDS – Narrow bands painted on the mast and boom to mark the maximum extension of the mainsail luff and foot.

BLOCK – A pulley.

BLOCK AND TACKLE – A multi-purchase pulley system.

BOLT ROPE – Rope sewn or enclosed in the luff of the mainsail.

BOOM – Spar attached to the foot of the mainsail – and sometimes the jib.

BOOM VANG – Multi-purchase system or lever, also known as a kicking strap, to prevent the boom from rising and to control the shape of the mainsail.

BOTTLE SCREW – Screw system used to tension rigging.

BOW – Front end of the dinghy.

BOWLINE – A knot used to tie a loop into the end of a rope.

BOWSPRIT – Spar that extends forward of the bow to support an asymmetric spinnaker on a dinghy.

BREAKWATER – Small upstanding ledge or coaming across the foredeck to deflect water.

BROACH – When a dinghy slews out of control broadside to the wind and sea.

BROAD REACH – Point of sail when wind is abaft the beam.

BULLSEYE – Wooden block or thimble with a hole drilled through it to take a rope to act as a block or stopper.

BULKHEAD – Transverse partition within the boat.

BUNG – Plug to block a drainage hole.

BUOY – Floating racing mark or navigation mark.

BUOYANCY – Power to float, having a density less than water.

BUOYANCY BAGS/TANKS – Built-in buoyancy to support the dinghy in the event of a capsize.

BURGEE – Small flag flown from the masthead.

C

CAM CLEAT – Cleat with two spring-load cams to hold a rope.

CAMBER – Curvature of a sail.

CAPSIZE – Point when the mast of a dinghy touches the water.

CATAMARAN – Twin-hulled vessel.

CENTRE OF BUOYANCY – Point where the buoyant force of water acts on the hull.

CENTRE OF EFFORT – Point where the force of wind acts on the rig.

CENTRE OF PRESSURE – Point where the side force of wind acts on the hull.

CENTREBOARD – Retractable keel that limits leeway, or the sideways force of the sails.

CHAIN PLATE – Hull or deck fitting to which the shroud is attached.

CHART – Map of the sea.

CHINE – Line or crease in the hull. A dinghy built from flat sheets of plywood is known as a hard chine boat.

CHINESE GYBE – Involuntary crash gybe.

CHORD DEPTH – Maximum depth of an aerofoil section.

CIRRUS – High-level cloud.

CIRROCUMULUS – High-level cloud.

CIRROSTRATUS – High-level cloud with little form.

CLAM CLEAT – Cleat with no moving parts that secures rope within its grooved, V-shaped body.

CLEAT – Fitting designed to hold a rope under tension without the use of a knot or hitch.

CLEVIS PIN – Pin that closes the fork of a rigging screw.

CLEW – Lower, aft corner of a sail.

CLEW OUTHAUL – Adjustor to change tension on the clew, and shape of the sail.

CLINKER CONSTRUCTION – Traditional form of hull construction where the planks overlap each other.

CLOSE REACH – Point of sailing midway between close-hauled and a beam reach.

CLOSE – HAULED – Point of sailing closest to wind.

CLOVE HITCH – Common knot or hitch used to tie a rope to a ring or rail.

COAMING – Small upstanding ledge or breakwater across or around the deck to deflect water.

COCKPIT – Area of the dinghy where helm and crew operate the boat.

COMPASS – Navigation instrument that points to the magnetic north pole.

CRINGLE – Metal eye or attachment point in each corner of the sail.

CUMULUS – Low-level cloud.

CUMULONIMBUS – Low-level rain cloud.

CUNNINGHAM HOLE – Cringle in luff to attach a purchase to flatten the sail.

CURRENT – A stream of water.

D

DACRON – American name for man-made sail material named polyester in Europe.

DAGGERBOARD – A vertically retracting keel that limits leeway, or the sideways force of the sails.

DEAD RUN – Sailing dead downwind.

DEPRESSION – Meteorological term for an area of low pressure.

DEVIATION – Compass error influenced by magnetic materials nearby.

DINGHY – Small open boat without a fixed keel.

DIRTY WIND – Disturbed wind or wind shadow effect from a dinghy to windward.

DISPLACEMENT – Volume/weight that a hull displaces in water.

DOWNHAUL – Rope or purchase used to tension the tack of a sail or Cunningham.

DOWNWIND – Sailing in the same direction as the wind.

E

EASE – To slacken a rope or let a sheet out.

EBB – Outgoing tide or flow.

EDDIES – Area of reverse or back-running current.

F

FAIRLEAD – A fixed lead to guide a rope or sheet and prevent chafe.

FAIRWAY – Main navigable channel.

FAIR WIND – Wind direction that allows a boat to sail from A to B without tacking.

FATHOM – Nautical unit of measure equal to 6ft (1.828m).

FENDER – Portable cushion or inflatable bladder to protect the hull from rubbing against another boat or a pontoon.

FETCH – Straight course sailed to windward without tacking.

FIGURE-OF-EIGHT KNOT – Stopper knot.

FOILS – Collective term for keel, centreboard/daggerboard and rudder.

FLOOD TIDE – A rising tide.

FOLLOWING WIND – Opposite of headwind, when the wind comes from astern.

FORESAIL – Jib.

FORESTAY – Forward stay supporting the mast.

FREEBOARD – Height of a boat's side above the water.

FRONT – Meteorological term describing a distinct line of weather – cold front, warm front etc.

FURL – To gather up or reef a sail in an orderly manner.

G

GAFF – Spar supporting the top of a traditional four-sided mainsail – gaff rig.

GATE START – Method of starting a race with fleet passing behind the stern of a guard boat tracking behind a dinghy sailing close-hauled on port tack.

GEL COAT – The smooth waterproof outer resin coating of a fibre-reinforced moulded hull and deck.

GENOA – Large headsail that overlaps the mainsail.

GNAV – Upward facing version of a vang or kicking strap used to prevent the boom from rising and control the shape of the mainsail.

GO ABOUT – To tack through the eye of the wind.

GOOSENECK – Double-hinged fitting to attach boom to mast.

GOOSE-WINGED – Running before the wind with mainsail set on one side and jib 'goose-winged' out on the other.

GPS – Satellite-based global positioning system.

GRADIENT WIND – Meteorological term caused by changes in barometric pressure. The greater the change in pressure, the steeper the gradient.

GRP – Glass reinforced plastic.

GUDGEON – Female part of a pair of rudder hangings into which the male pintle fits.

GUNTER RIG – Traditional high-aspect mainsail with gaff that extends almost vertically up from the mast.

GUNWALE – Outer strengthening piece around the top of the hull.

GUY – Windward spinnaker sheet or boom restrainer.

GYBE – Controlled form of tacking downwind when the transom passes through the eye of the wind and the boom flies across from one side to the other.

HALF HITCH – Temporary knot to attach a rope to a rail.

HALYARD – Rope or wire line to hoist sails up the mast.

HANK – Clip to attach luff or sail to a stay.

HARD CHINE – Line where the flat sheets used to construct a hull meet.

HARDEN UP – To point closer to wind.

HEAD – Top corner of a sail.

HEADBOARD – Reinforced top corner of a mainsail.

HEADING – Direction that a boat is taking.

HEADSAIL – Jib or genoa.

HEADSTAY – Forward stay supporting the mast.

HEAD TO WIND – Boat facing directly into wind - the no-go zone..

HEAVE TO – To bring the boat to a halt, head to wind, by backing the jib, putting the rudder down and letting the mainsail fly.

HEEL – Bottom end of the mast. The sideways tilt of a sailing boat.

HELM – Rudder. Also short for helmsman or helmsperson.

HIGHFIELD LEVER – A locking lever to tension stays.

HIKE – To sit out and counter the heeling force of the wind.

HITCH – Type of knot for attaching a rope to a rail or hoop.

HOIST – Vertical dimension of a sail or flag.

HOUNDS – Where the shrouds connect to the mast.

HOVE TO – See Heave to.

IMMINENT – Meteorological term for change in weather within six hours.

INGLEFIELD CLIPS – Interlocking C-shaped clips used to attach signal flaps, and sometimes a spinnaker, to a halyard.

IN IRONS – Term used when a sailboat is caught head to wind within the no-go zone.

ISOBAR – Meteorological term for line on weather map linking points of equal atmospheric pressure.

JIB – headsail.

JIB SHEETS – Ropes controlling the set of the jib.

JIB STICK – Pole to goose-wing the jib from when sailing dead downwind. Also known as a whisker pole.

JUMPER STAY – Stay on the foreside of the mast to limit the amount of bend in the spar.

KEDGE – Light, temporary anchor to hold the boat against an adverse tidal stream.

KICKING STRAP – Multi-purchase system or lever, also known as a vang, to prevent the boom from rising and control the shape of the mainsail.

KITE – Abbreviation for spinnaker.

KNOT – Nautical mile per hour (1 nautical mile equals 1.15 statute miles or 1,852m). Also refers to a rope tie.

KNUCKLE – Sharp longitudinal line of distortion within the hull.

LAND BREEZE – Offshore wind opposite to a sea breeze, that develops when the temperature of the sea is higher than the land.

LANYARD – Short length of cord used as a safety line.

LATERAL RESISTANCE – Ability of a boat to resist leeway or sideways force of the wind.

LEAD – The direction that a rope is led.

LEE – Opposite to windward. The side away from the wind.

LEECH – Trailing edge of a sail.

LEE BOW – Sailing on a tack where the tidal stream carries the boat towards the wind.

LEE HELM – A sailing boat, which requires its tiller to be pushed down to the leeward side to counter the boat's natural tendency to bear away, is said to carry 'lee helm'. This condition signifies that the rig is out of balance with the hull.

LEE HO – Final warning call of helm as the tiller is pushed over to leeward during a tack.

LEE SHORE – Shoreline which the wind is blowing towards.

LEEWARD – Opposite of windward; away from the wind.

LIFEJACKET – Buoyancy vest designed to keep a non-swimmer or unconscious person floating head up.

LIFT – A shift in the wind that swings aft. Otherwise known as a freeing wind.

LOA – Length overall.

LOOSE-FOOTED – Sail attached to a boom only by the clew and outhaul.

LUFF – The leading edge of a sail.

LUFFING – When a sailboat is steered closer to the wind.

LUFF ROPE – Rope sewn or enclosed in the luff of the mainsail. Also known as boltrope.

LWL – Load waterline or length of waterline.

Ⓜ

MAGNETIC NORTH – Compass heading.

MAGNETIC VARIATION – Difference in angle between true north and magnetic north.

MAINSAIL – Principal sail set on a mast.

MAINSHEET – Rope attached to the boom to trim the mainsail.

MAMMA – Dark low level rain cloud with udder-like shape.

MARLING HITCH – Line of linked knots tying sail to a spar.

MILLIBAR – Meteorological term for unit of pressure equal to 1/10000th of a bar.

MOULD – Male or female pattern for producing a plastic hull and other mouldings.

MULTIHULL – Generic term for a catamaran or trimaran.

MYLAR – Polyester film used in the manufacture of sails.

Ⓝ

NAUTICAL MILE – 1 nautical mile equals 1.15 statute miles or 1,852m.

NEAP TIDES – Tides with the smallest rise and fall. Opposite of spring tides.

NIMBO – Rain cloud.

NIMBOSTRATUS – Middle level rain cloud.

NO-GO ZONE – Area 40° either side of the direction of the wind.

Ⓞ

OCCLUDED FRONT – Meteorological term to describe when a cold front overtakes a warm front.

OFFSHORE WIND – Wind blowing seaward off the land.

OFFWIND – Sailing in the same direction as the wind.

OFF THE WIND – Sailing a course lower than a beam reach.

ONSHORE WIND – Wind blowing inland off the sea.

ON THE WIND – Sailing a close-hauled course.

OOD – Officer of the Day.

OUTHAUL – Line used to stretch the clew of a sail to the end of the boom.

Ⓟ

PAINTER – Mooring line.

PELICAN HOOK – Metal hook with a cam-action lock.

PFD – Personal flotation device such as a buoyancy aid or lifejacket.

PINCH – Sailing so close to the wind that the sails start to luff and lose drive.

PINTLE – Male part of a pair of rudder hangings that fits into the female gudgeon.

PITCHPOLE – When a boat capsizes end over end.

PLANING – When a boat lifts its bows out of the water, and because of the reduced drag, then accelerates onto to a planing attitude.

POLED OUT – Running before the wind with mainsail set on one side and the jib poled out or 'goose-winged' on the other.

POINTS OF SAILING – Beating, reaching and running before the wind.

PORT – Left hand side of a boat.

PORT GYBE – Sailing downwind with the wind on the port side of the boat and mainsail out to port. This is the give-way gybe.

PORT TACK – Sailing with the wind on the port (left) side of the boat. This is the give-way tack.

PORTSMOUTH YARDSTICK – Simple dinghy handicapping system when mixed classes race together.

PRE-BEND – Amount of fore and aft bend set in a mast.

PREVENTER – Safety line.

PURCHASE – Mechanical advantage of the block and tackle or lever.

Q

QUARTER – Sides of the boat aft, i.e. starboard quarter, port quarter.

R

RACE – Fast running tide or stream.

RACING FLAG/PENNANT – Small rectangular flag flown at the masthead to signal that the boat is racing.

RAKE – Degree that a mast leans back from vertical.

RATCHET BLOCK – Purchase block with an integral ratchet to lessen the load of a sheet held in the hand.

REACH – Sailing course with the wind abeam.

REACHING – Sailing with the wind abeam.

REACHING HOOK – Device set close to the shrouds to run the windward spinnaker sheet or guy through.

READY ABOUT – First warning call to the crew that the helm intends to tack.

REEF – To reduce or shorten sail.

REEF KNOT – Knot joining two ropes together.

RHUMB LINE – Straight line between two points drawn on a Mercator chart.

RIDING TURN – When a rope or sheet crosses under itself and jams, most often around a winch.

RIG – General term for mast, spars and sails.

RIGGING – Standing wires that hold up the mast.

RIGGING SCREW – Screw to tension shrouds. Also known as a bottle screw.

RIGHT OF WAY – Term within Collision Regulations denoting a boat with rights, as opposed to a boat that must give way.

ROACH – The top curve within the leech of a mainsail.

ROCKER – Fore and aft curve within the central underside sections of the boat.

ROLL TACKING – Use of crew weight to speed the process of tacking to windward.

ROLLER JIB – Furling headsail.

ROTATING MAST – Spar designed to rotate from port to starboard to present its best aspect to the wind.

ROUND TURN AND TWO HALF HITCHES – Knot used to attach rope to a rail or hoop.

RUBBING STRAKE – A strengthening strip secured to the gunwale as a protective buffer.

RUDDER – Moving foil to steer the boat with.

RUN – Sailing dead downwind.

RUNNING BY THE LEE – Sailing downwind with the mainsail set on the windward side and about to gybe.

RUNNING RIGGING – Sheets and halyards used to set and control the sails.

S

SEA BREEZE – Onshore wind opposite to a land breeze, that develops when the temperature of the land is higher than the sea.

SELF BAILER – Thru-hull bailer that, once activated, allows the bilge water to flow out when the dinghy is planing.

SHACKLE – Metal link with screw pin to connect wires and lines.

SHEAVE – The wheel within a block.

SHEET – Any rope used to adjust sail shape.

SHEET BEND – Knot used to join two dissimilar sized ropes together.

SHOCK CORD – Elastic or bungee cord made of rubber strands.

SHROUDS – Wires supporting either side of the mast.

SLAB REEF – Method of reefing the mainsail.

SLIP LINE – Temporary double line with both ends made fast to the boat that can be released from onboard and pulled in.

SLOT EFFECT – The effect a jib has in accelerating the flow of air around the back of a mainsail.

SNAP SHACKLE – Shackle with a secure locking mechanism instead of a pin.

SPAR – General term for a mast, boom, gaff or spinnaker pole.

SPINNAKER – Large parachute-like downwind sail.

SPINNAKER CHUTE – Open-mouthed tubular container fitted in the bow of a dinghy from which to launch and recover the spinnaker.

SPINNAKER POLE – Spar to set the spinnaker from.

SPREADER – A strut usually fitted in pairs to deflect the shrouds and control the bending characteristics of the mast.

SPRING TIDE – Extreme high tide caused by the gravitational pull of the moon.

STAND ON BOAT – Right of way boat.

SQUALL – Sudden, short-lived increase in wind.

STARBOARD – Right hand side of the boat.

STARBOARD GYBE – Sailing downwind with the wind on the starboard side of the boat and mainsail out to port. This is the right-of-way gybe.

STARBOARD TACK – Sailing upwind with the wind on the starboard side of the boat and mainsail out to port. This is the right-of-way tack.

STAY – Forward mast support.

STEM – Forward extremity of the boat.

STERN – Aft extremity of the boat.

STOPPER – A cleating device that holds a sheet or halyard fast.

STRATUS – Featureless low-level cloud.

STRATOCUMULUS – Low-level cloud.

STROP – A ring of rope or wire used to make up an attachment to a spar.

SWIVEL – Connector whose two parts rotate.

SWIVEL BLOCK – Block with a swivel joint.

T

TABERNACLE – Structure supporting a deck-stepped mast.

TACK – Lower forward corner of a sail.

TACKING – To sail close-hauled through the eye of the wind.

TACKLE – Multi-purchase system.

TAIL – The free end of a sheet or halyard.

TALURIT – Swaged wire splice.

TELLTALES – Strips of fabric or wool attached to the luff of a jib and leech of the mainsail to indicate airflow across the sail.

THWART – Transverse seat or plank amidships.

TIDAL STREAM – Flow of water caused by the rise and fall of tide.

TIDE – Six-hourly rise and fall of water caused by the gravitational pull of the moon.

TILLER – Arm of a rudder to control boat direction.

TILLER EXTENSION – Lightweight pole with universal joint attached to the end of the tiller to allow the helm to sit outboard or steer from the trapeze.

TOE STRAPS – Lengths of webbing running fore and aft in a dinghy for crew to hook their feet under and hike out.

TRAILING EDGE – Aft edge of a foil, i.e. sail, keel, rudder etc.

TRAINING RUN – Sailing downwind 5-10° shy of the dead downwind angle.

TRAMPOLINE – Rope netting or webbing strung between two hulls of a catamaran.

TRANSIT – Sighting two objects in line.

TRANSOM – Transverse aft end of a boat.

TRANSOM FLAP – Flaps that open at the stern to allow water to escape from a planing dinghy following a capsize.

TRAPEZE – Harness attached by wire to the hounds of the mast to allow the crew to extend their whole body outboard of the dinghy to improve their righting moment.

TRAVELLER – Fitting on a rope or track with limited

travel used to adjust the mainsheet.

TRIM – To adjust the sails to suit the wind direction.

TRIMARAN – Three-hulled multihull.

TRUE WIND – Direction and velocity of wind measured at a stationary position.

TWIST – Difference in angle to the wind between the top and bottom of a sail.

UNIVERSAL JOINT – Hinge that allows universal movement.

UNSTAYED MAST – Mast without standing rigging.

UPHAUL – Control line to adjust the height of the spinnaker pole.

UPWIND – Any course closer to the wind than a beam reach.

VANG – Multi-purchase system or lever, also known as a kicking strap, to prevent the boom from rising and control the shape of the mainsail.

VARIATION – Difference in angle between true north and magnetic north.

VMG – Velocity made good to windward.

WAKE – Turbulence left astern of a moving boat.

WARP – Rope used to moor a boat.

WEATHER HELM – A sailing boat, which requires its tiller to be held up towards the weather side to counter the boat's natural tendency to luff, is said to carry 'weather helm'. This condition signifies that the rig is out of balance with the hull.

WEATHER SHORE – Shoreline where the wind is blowing offshore.

WETTED SURFACE – Total underwater area of the hull.

WHISKER POLE – Pole to goose-wing the jib from when sailing dead downwind. Also known as a jib stick.

WINCH – Capstan used to tension sail sheets and halyards.

WINDAGE – Drag caused by the boat and crew.

WINDWARD – Towards the wind; opposite of leeward.

WIND GRADIENT – Difference in wind speed close to the water and a certain height above it such as the masthead. This is not the same as gradient wind, which refers to changes in barometric pressure.

WINDLASS – See winch.

WORKING END – End of a rope used to tie a knot.

Index

Acknowledgements

Our thanks to UKSA who have assisted with the production of this book. They have answered questions and been a sounding board on many areas. A charity based in Cowes, UKSA is dedicated to changing lives through maritime activity, and trains almost 6,000 people every year from all backgrounds and at all levels. From children as young as 8 years old learning watersports skills, to the full range of RYA qualifications, and up to MCA Master 300gt, UKSA is an expert in the watersports and yacht training industry. (*www.uksa.org*).

We must also thank Chris Tunstall and his team at Performance Laser for allowing the use of the Laser family of dinghies to provide realism to the illustrations, and to illustrator Greg Filip who worked so hard to faithfully reproduce the methodology taught by the UKSA.

David Houghton, the former weather guru to Britain's Olympic sailing team and author of *Weather at Sea* also provided valued advice.

Grateful thanks also go to Emma Brenton and Bryan Benjafield, the picture research team at PPL Photo Agency, for sourcing the many photographs we required to illustrate particular points throughout the book.

Credits:
All illustrations: *Greg Filip/PPL* Photo Research: *PPL Photo Agency*. Photographs: *Peter Bentley/PPL*: 28, 76, 130, 170, 179. *Matias Capizzano*/PPL: 25, 152, 153, 154, 156, 158, 160/1, 163. *Jo Clegg*/PPL: 75. *Graham Franks*/PPL: 75. *David Freeman*/PPL: 74. *Neal Grundy*/PPL: 36, 37, 38, 39. *Nick Kirk*/PPL: 27, 71, 78, 118. *Alberto Mariotti*/PPL: 77. *Jon Nash*/PPL: 79, 87. *Performance Laser:* pages 6/7, 8, 9, 20, 23, 24, 29, 59, 90/91, 136 *Barry Pickthall/PPL:* 9, 21, 22, 30, 31, 32, 33, 34, 35, 36, 37, 38, 39, 40, 41, 42/3, 44/5, 46, 47, 48, 49, 50, 51, 53, 54, 55, 58, 61, 73, 108, 109, 110, 111, 116/7, 119, 121, 124, 138, 140, 141, 143, 144, 145, 146, 147, 148, 149, 150, 158. *PPL Photo Agency:* 74, 77. *Dave Porter/PPL:* 76. *Roy Roberts/PPL:* 73 *OnEdition/OC Events:* 88. *UKSA:* 26, 50, 56.

ENJOYABLE TRAINING & QUALIFICATIONS

Free guidance and advice
Just call +44 (0) 1983 203034

RVA Training Centre

Visit www.uksa.org

UKSA